LEADING
WOMEN

LEADING WOMEN

20 Influential Women
Share Their Secrets to

LEADERSHIP, BUSINESS, AND LIFE

NANCY D. O'REILLY, PSYD

Avon, Massachusetts

Published by
Adams Media, a division of F+W Media, Inc.
57 Littlefield Street, Avon, MA 02322. U.S.A.
www.adamsmedia.com

ISBN 10: 1-4405-8417-6
ISBN 13: 978-1-4405-8417-6
eISBN 10: 1-4405-8418-4
eISBN 13: 978-1-4405-8418-3

Printed in the United States of America.

10 9 8 7 6 5 4 3 2

Dedication

This book is for my daughters Lauren, Leigh, and Ragan; my granddaughters Alexis, Isabel, Dain, PJ, Sky, Raven, and Aspen; my grandson Tristan; and my great-grandson Julian.

Acknowledgments

So many people have helped birth this book. I want to thank:

- My nineteen contributing authors, each one committed to supporting our sisterhood. They all wholeheartedly shared their passion and talents to make women stronger and more powerfully able to change the world for good.
- My dream team that makes me look good. Maggie Castrey, editor, mentor, friend, you are the director and orchestrator of this book, for your diligence, tenacity, calm, and constant belief that we would complete this book; Cathy Evans, producer and writer, for your passion, care, concern, and writing flair; Sherry Haney, webmaster and Internet guru, for keeping us seen, heard, and looking good online; Melissa Miller Young and Cory Goode, who spin social media to bring new members to our community and spread our message.
- My family and friends, who cheer me on with their belief that all things are possible.
- My high school counselor, who set me on fire by telling me to forget about college and look into secretarial school.
- My creator and all the masters and angels who are with me each day; especially my guardian angels, my mother, Phyllis, and my grandmothers, Anna and Mama Nancy. I'm trying my best to fill your shoes today as the earthly Mama Nancy.

Many blessings to you. We are all in this together, working to build a world in which women and girls have social, political, and economic rights and equality with men and boys.

CONTENTS

Part Three:
Connecting to Support Each Other 139

INTRODUCTION

What an incredible time to be a woman! Never before have women been so powerful. Yet, for many of us, our relationship with power continues to be fraught with insecurity, ambivalence, and confusion. We want it but do not know how to get it and are afraid to admit we seek it. When we have it, we hide it. We are often afraid to use it because our society punishes powerful women in subtle and not-so-subtle ways.

Our relationship with power bewilders us, which is why I wanted to create this book. We need to sort out our mixed feelings about power so we can get it, claim it, and use it to create a better world. In addition, we should have a wonderful time creating power for ourselves, and feeling connected with the sisterhood of smart, amazing women. How is that for a tall order?

Women are well on their way to claiming power. In just ten generations, women have become more or less equal to men under the law. We currently attain more college degrees than men and hold the highest government office in several lands. Women's organized efforts have developed the hospitals, schools, museums, libraries, and social supports that enrich the civilized life of our communities. Everywhere you look groups of women are organizing community support for those who need it, solving problems, and addressing issues that need a woman's touch.

That is very good news, worthy of a champagne toast to our smart, determined foremothers who marched and raised their voices to achieve these gains. However, we all know it is not the whole story. While we have accomplished much in just a few decades, women as a whole still do not exercise power in ways that are equal to men's.

11

In the United States, women still earn less than men (averaging seventy-eight cents to a man's dollar). Women fill few government leadership roles and occupy fewer than 20 percent of corporate C-level jobs. The majority of American women work outside the home, yet they still take an ever greater responsibility than their partners do for household and family chores. The Equal Rights Amendment was introduced in 1923, and after failing to meet its ratification deadline in 1982, it is still not a law—so women's rights are not yet protected under the U.S. Constitution. Even worse, millions of women all over the world still lack basic human rights and are subjected to violence at staggering rates. It is very clear that women's work is not yet done.

Women of the post–World War II baby boom famously worked for change in the sixties (many continue to do so today), and younger women are also rising to the cause. Sheryl Sandberg, COO of Facebook, pursues her mission to help women overcome obstacles within themselves, and she urges us to sit at the table. Like many women, Sheryl has downplayed her success throughout her life, accurately perceiving that successful women pay a popularity penalty. (In contrast, success boosts men's popularity.)

Sheryl discovered that finding her voice and speaking out helped her overcome a lot of her insecurities. Examples include her TED Talk at the TEDWomen 2010 conference, her book *Lean In: Women, Work, and the Will to Lead*, and her LeanIn .org foundation. Her book sold more than 150,000 copies in its first week and has been on the nonfiction bestseller list ever since. Her clear messages: (1) women should strongly pursue their ambitions instead of putting on the brakes, and (2) women need to make their spouses truly equal partners at home. The result, she declares, will be more profitable businesses, healthier families, and better communities for all of us.

Although Sheryl's book is inspiring, it offers few specific tools. That is where *this* book comes in. I asked nineteen other veteran thought leaders to tell us, "What are the keys women must acquire if they are to unlock their personal power and create a better world?" The answers to this question provide insights for translating ideas into action. I have also added my own thoughts regarding this question, which you will find at the end of Part Two.

I created the WomenConnect4Good.org foundation with the mission to help women ignite their lives and connect with each other to change our world. This book is a continuation of that vision. I've had so much fun working on social-profit (nonprofit) projects with other women throughout my life, and it has been an honor to create positive change for women, children, and families.

This book provides tools for making your voice heard and for gaining the respect and opportunities you need to claim your rightful place, shape your life, provide for your family, and invent a better society. Our authors show how women's leadership benefits the world, and they list the qualities, skills, and events that help women create change. Most inspiring of all, they provide examples of women working together with others to create change today.

When you read about a great technique in the following pages, apply it in your own life and then share it with another woman. Let's create a world in which every woman is able to claim her power, see her advice and expertise valued and respected, conquer her internal barriers, and work together with other women and men. If the hand that rocks the cradle is ever going to help rule the world, it must reach out to clasp another hand. What steps will you take today to tip the scales permanently toward this better world?

Part One

Mastering Our External Environment

A woman must exercise courage to push herself forward into a world that often feels unwelcoming if not outright hostile. One thing is certain, without the support and encouragement of our sisterhood, few of us would carry on. While you do this important work, remember to take the time to bring your women friends together to celebrate your successes.

The authors in this first section offer specific tools and techniques in their answers to my question, "What are the keys women must acquire if they are to unlock their personal power and create a better world?" Each of these authors is a thought leader in her profession who works to inspire and educate other women. After reading and adopting the strategies in this section, you will feel more comfortable exercising your power so that you can move forward confidently to achieve your goals.

As women sharpen their skills, they will continue to advance in the former off-limit areas of corporate business and government. Look around you. Reach out to other like-minded women in your world so you can help each other. When a woman meets success using her feminine skills, she can and should help others learn to do the same thing. Together, we can accomplish the powerful results we want to achieve.

From Oppression to Leadership: Women Redefine Power

by Gloria Feldt
Cofounder and president of Take the Lead

"We will shift from the oppressive, outdated, patriarchal model of 'power-over' to an expansive model of 'power-to' that transforms how we lead, and how we live."

What is your relationship to power? On a scale of one to ten, with one being, "I don't like the idea of power so I don't seek it," ten being, "I love having power," and the middle range being, "I'm not so comfortable with power, but I know I need to deal with it," where do you place yourself?

I recently keynoted a conference of two hundred of the most powerful women lawyers and judges in the country. Not one of them raised her hand when I asked who rated herself a perfect "ten." A few hands went up at the other end of the scale, ones or twos. Most hands raised in the five-to-seven range. After a few minutes discussing the question, one table of women burst out in laughter. "We agreed we could own up to being nines," they told the group, "but ten just seemed too pushy."

I wasn't surprised. I see this bell curve in almost every predominantly female group. Men are far more likely to claim to be tens without hesitation. In one mixed group, a man, trying to be encouraging, chided a young woman who pegged herself as a two, whereupon she curled up into a fetal position in her beanbag chair and I had to coax her back into the conversation.

In another example, a colleague conducted a focus group of executive women to learn their preferences for a leadership course she was developing. These women were leaders in their respective professions or companies. When my colleague threw out ideas for names of the leadership program, those containing the word *power* drew the most controversy. One participant said she did not like the word because "it speaks to dominance." Another said the program should not use "power" because "it is highly offensive to some people."

I started studying women's relationship with power in 2008, when it appeared we might have our first female president. I wrote an article for *Elle* magazine about women in politics, assuming it would be an optimistic look at how women are ascending to elective office. How surprised I was to learn, however, that at the rate we were progressing, it would take another seventy years for women to achieve parity in Congress.

Whether we are talking work, politics, or personal life, the dynamics of power are the same.

Women currently represent 51 percent of the population, 57 percent of college graduates, half the workplace, and 54 percent of voters, but only hold 18 percent of the top leadership positions across all sectors. Despite the potential power of sheer numbers in all these areas, we have barely moved the dial toward meaningful leadership parity in the last two decades.

The business case for women in leadership is clear: more women equal greater profits. Yet the *2013 Catalyst Census* reports found women flatlined again compared to the previous year's 14.6 percent of executive officer positions in *Fortune* 500 companies and 16.9 percent overall of board seats—the eighth year in a row of no appreciable increase.

Many efforts (some of them listed here) aim to change the gender ratio in leadership. One blog called *change:the:ratio* focuses on gender equality in the tech world and social media. Vision 2020 at Drexel University College of Medicine works across all sectors. Thousands of women's leadership programs attract hundreds of thousands of women each year. Facebook COO Sheryl Sandberg's Lean In initiative gives women, especially in corporate America, much encouragement to stay in the game even when the work environment feels hostile. *Women Don't Ask* authors Linda Babcock and Sara Laschever teach negotiating skills, after documenting that the gender pay gap can be attributed to women's reticence to self-advocate and negotiate aggressively for raises and promotions. This reluctance to ask costs each of us a cool half million dollars or more over a lifetime's earnings.

Nonpartisan groups like the Women's Campaign Forum and the White House Project and partisan groups such as Emily's List (Democratic) and the Wish List (Republican) have long attempted with minimal success to get more women to run for office. When a woman runs, she is as likely as a man to win. She is as able to raise money and starts with greater voter trust than male candidates—which after partisan gridlock and numbing scandals featuring the likes of Spitzer, Weiner, Sanford, and Petraeus is hardly eyebrow-raising news.

It became clear to me that the problem is no longer external barriers and biases holding women back, though those certainly still exist. Women now have the necessary resources and the power to move forward; and the world is crying out for women's leadership.

Power unused is power useless.

That is why I recently cofounded Take the Lead (find it at *www.TakeTheLeadWomen.com*). To break through the logjam and speed progress toward parity, women must transform our own relationship with power. When women change the way we think about power, we will then shift from the oppressive, outdated, patriarchal model of "power-over" to an expansive model of "power-to" that transforms how we lead and how we live.

There are good reasons for women's ambivalence about embracing power. We must understand them in order to progress. First, political scientist Jennifer Lawless, author of *It Takes a Candidate*, attributes the deficit of women in political office to a deficit of ambition. But the more I dug into the research, interviewed women across the country, and looked into my own heart and performance as a leader, the more I came to attribute the disparity not to lack of ambition but to women's socialization that leads to less intention. Ambition is aspirational—having a goal, hope, or desire. Intention implies assuming you are empowered to achieve your ambition and that you take the responsibility to make it happen. Boys are typically socialized from birth to see the world as their oyster and have no reticence about claiming their power. Girls are typically raised to attune themselves first to the needs of others, to respond rather than assume their own agency, even though today they are simultaneously told they can become anything they want to be.

Second, women have been discriminated against; we have been raped; we have had countless bad things happen to us because people have had power over us. These experiences have created so much pain that we know we do not want to receive the oppressive kind of power. Sexism is merely a form of humiliation in order to assert power-over. Sexism belittles and diminishes, whether by denial (the right to vote, equal seats in the corporate boardroom) or false elevation (the gilded cage, the pedestal).

Third, the belief that power is a finite pie; when you take a slice, there is less for me. While we're well past the time when brawn alone ruled the social order (and physical strength was the measure of power), the notion that if a woman has power, there's less for the man still lurks in the recesses of our prehensile minds. Moreover, women who assume powerful positions by merely adopting male models of power and leadership do not advance the cause of equality.

Fourth, it is hard to change a culture while you are living in it. It is challenging to see injustices, just as fish cannot see the water they swim in. In addition, it is risky—changing power structures changes relationships, and women may fear losing relationships they value.

For all these reasons, women may shy away from power. However, when I suggest we redefine power as the power to accomplish their goals, women respond, "Yes, I want that kind of power!" Power-to lets you innovate and make the world a better place for yourself, your family, your community, and the world. Power-to is possibility. Power-over makes you feel powerless. Power-to lets you feel powerful. I like the quote by Audre Lorde,

"When I dare to be powerful—to use my strength in the service of my vision, then it becomes less and less important whether I am afraid." Power-over is oppression. Power-to is leadership. A leader needs her power tools.

There is not space here to share all nine of the power tools I created in *No Excuses: Nine Ways Women Can Change How We Think about Power*. My greatest pleasure is conducting workshops where we have the chance to practice all of them. So I will share one power tool that is probably the most singularly effective in women's quest for equality and leadership parity. It's No Excuses Power Tool #2:

Define your own terms— first, before someone else defines you. Because we are all going to be defined. Branded. Named. Framed in culture, media, and language. All language is ultimately the discourse of power.

Here are four tips to help you define your terms.

1. **Be intentional.** Whoever sets the terms of the debate usually wins it. Whoever sets the agenda usually gets what she wants accomplished in the meeting. Women are generally smart enough not to be interested in attaining

power for its own sake—to wield power over others just because it is there for the taking. Nevertheless, to get things done, we must think proactively and intentionally about what we want to have happen, and then frame the conversation so that it will happen.

2. **Be fluent in the language of power.** This requires women to become, in a sense, bilingual—to speak male as well as female language. Because men still control most of the clout positions, women must be able to communicate successfully across both communication styles, while retaining authenticity. For example, men tend to ask directly for what they want rather than hoping indirect statements will be interpreted correctly. Speaking in simple, declarative sentences and avoiding "upspeak," which makes it sound as though one's declarative sentences are questions, are simple techniques to communicate power and confidence. It is perfectly legitimate for women to expect men to reciprocate by learning to understand and appreciate female communication styles, too. In our increasingly diverse world, it can only benefit all men and women to become more fluent in the nuances of gender language patterns just as they are becoming more fluent in the language patterns of their colleagues around the globe.

3. **Say the first word.** Set the tone for the conversation. Be poised, prepared, and ready to say the first word in any debate or meeting. Do not hesitate or wait just to be polite. Do not apologize for what you are about to say, or for having ideas or expectations, and do not sound like you are apologizing by ending every sentence with

an intonation rise as though it were a question. You are ready—so dive in. No Excuses.

4. **Say the last word.** If you are in a tough discussion, stick with it to the end. Speak with authority and clarity. Make eye contact. That does not mean to be rude or pushy, or that you should not seek input from others. Continue to use those simple declarative sentences referenced earlier and ask straightforward questions, actively listening to answers. Do not hedge your words or append endless qualifiers to your arguments. Speak your piece to your satisfaction.

Practical tools like these enable us to shift from a culture of oppression to a culture of positive intention, to make life better for everyone. We are on the right side of history. We can choose power over fear. By changing our relationship with power and redefining it from the oppressive power-over to the expansive power-to, we can embrace it to lead authentically as women. We can go with intention—in equal partnership with men—toward solutions that allow everyone to thrive with the freedom, peace, and prosperity that we all deserve.

The Power of the Podium: Challenges and Opportunities to Be Seen and Heard

by Lois Phillips, PhD
Speaker, educator, college administrator,
consultant, trainer, and coach

"Silence is not golden . . .
when men do all the talking."

Women today want a place at the head of the table and not just a seat. To advance into positions of power and influence, a women's place must be at the podium. After all, dynamic speakers provide a vision of a better future and inspire and initiate change efforts. Providing visibility and status, the podium is the place for emerging leaders to be seen, heard, and remembered.

Anxiety about public speaking remains common to both men and women. Sociologist Barbara Ehrenreich labeled it "public freaking" in *Ms. Magazine* in 1989 and Santa Barbara journalist Sheila Murphy wrote in 1999, "Most people would rather be in the casket than standing next to it and talking to the mourners." Women leaders need to do more than master their anxiety and gain basic presentation skills. They must become proactive, seeking and embracing every possible opportunity to speak to groups and then develop a dynamic style. After all, the podium provides an opportunity to cast a wide net. In today's web-centric world, a speaker's interesting remarks can echo beyond the conference room and become the basis for a quote or a news article, a Facebook post, an eBlast, and a tweet. As a result, remarks at the podium cannot be casual or impulsive because, unlike a conversation with a friend, you cannot take it back in the morning.

Delivering a presentation that achieves its purpose can be personally empowering. In planning her remarks, the speaker must ask herself:

- What do I stand for?
- What do I believe?
- Am I willing to take the heat for asserting my ideas and opinions?

Once she can answer these questions, the speaker is well prepared for the next set of unique challenges that lie ahead.

Women's Place, Women's Voices

Women today earn more bachelor's degrees than men do, are in nontraditional and managerial roles in the workplace, and are entering professions like law and medicine in numbers equal to men. Yet, incredibly, men are still largely in charge of major social systems. The statistics are surprising, a reminder of how far women need to go:

- Only 4.2 percent of the CEOs of *Fortune* 500 corporations are women.
- In Harvard's January 2013 *Business Review*, of the top 100 CEOs only 1.9 percent were women.

- Twenty-three percent of college presidents in the United States are women.
- Only twenty women are now in the U.S. Senate and eighty-one in the House.
- There are only five women state governors, down from six in 2012.

Too few executive women walk the hallowed halls of power.

The media perpetuates stereotypical images of how leaders should look and sound. Few women are depicted at the helm of a ship or navigate the Ship of State as a commanding presence. In reality, most CEOs are six feet tall and about 30 percent are over six foot two inches. No matter what, the average five-foot-four-inch woman will not fit the suit. Female CEOs average five foot nine inches in height (above the average female height). Perhaps that's why Senator Barbara Boxer—at four foot eleven inches—climbs a step stool at the podium. Her assertive speaking style, providing stature through eloquence, compensates for her lack of height.

In broadcast news, the "voice of authority" remains a male voice. The number of women interviewed as "experts" is surprisingly low, even at progressive NPR (according to an NPR ombudsman self-study). Of the twelve outside commentators who appeared at least twenty times each during a period of fifteen months, the only woman heard was political commentator Cokie Roberts (fifty-one times). Moreover, while viewers are more accustomed to seeing a woman as a news anchor, according to a study from Indiana University published in *Communication Research* in 2011, "the sexual attractiveness of female news anchors distracts men from remembering the news content." We can only assume that the same kind of distraction-phenomenon holds true for women at the podium. Remember the first time you were surprised to see a woman enter the cockpit and realize that she was the pilot? Attitudes change more slowly than reality.

Double Standard, Double Bind

Audiences have a psychological bias in favor of men as speakers. After all, society expects men to be rational and logical, see the big picture, and have goals outside of their roles as fathers. Nobody is surprised when a man takes the floor and begins to talk. And talk. And talk. Research confirms that male senators speak more than women senators do. Many people expect men to voice opinions but are critical of women who do.

Listeners want a speaker to project his voice adequately so that he is loud enough to be heard in the back of the room, but a woman who speaks in a loud voice is judged to be aggressive or too masculine. In a 2013 experiment at Yale about women and power, women posing as female CEOs were judged more harshly for voicing opinions too ardently while men posing as CEOs were perceived as poor leaders if they *did not* voice their opinions. Speaking up puts women in a double bind position: damned if you do, damned if you don't.

Simply put, women cannot be perceived as both feminine and a strong public speaker at the same time.

When it comes to showing emotion, we give men more latitude, even though women are thought to be innately more emotional. For instance, the double standard allows Congressman John Boehner to cry uncontrollably at press conferences without criticism while the mere presence of a (possible) tear seriously hurt presidential candidate Hillary Clinton's campaign. Women must project the image of a rational leader by being strategic about when, where, and how much they express their feelings.

Clearly, public speaking is a riskier endeavor for women than men. To paraphrase a popular book title, a woman speaker must be willing to "feel the fear and say it anyway." Every time she takes the stage or a seat at the head of the table, a woman speaker is transcending conventional attitudes toward the woman's role and the woman's place. Four empowering strategies will increase self-confidence at the podium:

Flaunt Your Track Record

At the podium men are believed to have credibility as leaders to start with but women have to earn it. That is why a woman needs to immediately convince listeners that she is an exceptional person. Her meta-message is: "I'll tell you the truth. You can trust me. I know what I'm talking about."

Building credibility requires women speakers to flaunt their expertise and character, something that may be difficult for any woman who has been raised on a modesty ethos, and for whom modesty is an aspect of femininity. For example, feminine women avoid talking about achievements in a way that might smack of self-congratulation or bragging. For women in today's competitive world, it is better to think of bragging as branding. *You are your brand.* People need to leave with your elevator speech at the tip of their tongue.

Women speakers have to also address the audience's skepticism about their ability to lead change. Nagging questions can interfere with the listener's ability to pay full attention to the content, even though they are questions that would never be an issue about a male speaker. Are you ready for prime time? Skeptical listeners are wondering:

- Can she make tough decisions? Is she emotionally strong enough? Can she handle pushback and conflicts?
- Can she mobilize resources? Is she connected to "old boys'" or women's networks? Is she a player?
- Is she capable of following up on promises she is making? Can she deliver?
- Can she stay focused on the big picture or will the details bog her down?
- Will she try to please everyone or can she remain decisive and action-oriented?
- Is she brainy enough to handle the complexity of today's high-tech global economy?

At the same time the speaker is preparing her key message points, she must be able to weave answers to these questions in her introductory remarks or presentation, providing specific concrete examples of achievements.

Introductory remarks create expectations, but they are often problematic: too long, read directly from a resume or the printed program, or delivered off-the-cuff—where they can be off-point or flippant. People must be clear about why you are at the podium speaking on your particular topic. Why not take control by preparing and providing the moderator with a Speaker Introduction cheat sheet? When there is a printed program, provide a written list of specific successes that reinforce your expertise, and e-mail it to the person preparing it. What you have accomplished is far more interesting than where you went to school or how many years you worked in your field. Your message must be, "I know what I'm talking about. This talk will change your life!"

Share the Stage

When Yahoo!'s CEO, Marissa Mayer, spoke at a Forbes conference, she made sure that she surprised the audience by adding high-powered celebrities to her presentation, including respected anchor Katie Couric and former *New York Times* tech editor, David Pogue, both of whom now work for Yahoo! You can also extend your reach by adding layers of voices to your presentation by including respected colleagues or experts, board members, or partners. When they endorse your project or product in a public venue, they create a "wow" moment, increasing your credibility as a leader and enhancing your power and authority.

Learn from Outspoken Women Who Can Take the Heat

Stick your neck out in public to confront the status quo and you might well become a target for criticism. Women leaders with strong opinions must prepare for pushback. Nobody with a thin skin will survive an onslaught of negative feedback, but other strong women have learned how to handle pushback, and some have even benefited from the publicity.

Former secretary of state Hillary Clinton is used to taking the heat. Possibly the most famous woman in the world with a 67 percent popularity rating, Clinton spent five hours being hazed and insulted during a 2013 congressional testimony about the terrorist attacks in Benghazi. Finally, after being repeatedly interrupted by a senator, she allowed herself to get angry, stood her ground, and made her point. "Four Americans are dead. . . . I take full responsibility," she said.

Michelle Obama talks to children and parents at public schools about her Let's Move! campaign to fight childhood obesity. But critics berate her for trying to change what parents put in a lunchbox. With a doctorate in political science, outspoken liberal journalist Rachel Maddow, the first openly gay TV host, uses her celebrity to be a paid professional speaker. Critical of misrepresentation in the media, she has angered many at Fox TV, where anchor Tricia Macke in November 2012 disparaged her professionalism, calling her "an angry young man." Clinton, Obama, and Maddow are diverse role models who know how to maintain their cool under fire. Their actions clearly say, "Take a stand, hold your ground, and never apologize for who you are and what you believe."

Consider that your remarks could be recorded, posted on YouTube, and circle the globe, so say what you mean and mean what you say. There is no taking it back.

When political policy is sexist, challenging the establishment can be dangerous. As an example, Pakistani schoolgirl Malala Yousafzai spoke boldly at the press club in Peshawar when she was only eleven years old, asking, "How dare the Taliban take away my basic right to education?" Four years later, she was shot in the head while riding her school bus home. Miraculously she survived and garnered global attention as a result. Malala has already become an icon and is immortalized as the youngest person nominated for the Nobel Peace Prize.

Connect with Your Audience

At the podium, women speakers have several advantages over men. Some feminine traits can be speaker strengths, such as respect for other people's opinions and a desire for connection. In general, research has found that women talk to exchange information and establish cohesion. They remain open to what the audience has to say in response to their ideas. Women speakers tend to provide information to help listeners achieve their goals, rather than to establish dominance over the group or negotiate status. And if listeners become restless, women speakers can quickly change course because at the podium—as well as in everyday life—women read nonverbal cues better than men do.

Women relate to friends through personal narratives, which can create a sense of intimacy. As well, audiences enjoy hearing a speaker share a cultural lesson or epiphany learned from an exotic trip. For women, a personal experience can be educational and politicizing. As an example, I heard a speaker who had been in a caregiver role head off a policy talk by answering her own question, "What have you learned about our health-care system from caring for a loved one with a chronic illness?" Her candor quickly engaged the audience's attention.

The personal stories we tell at the podium need to be succinct, tied to a main point, and not told for dramatic effect, for shock value, or to elicit sympathy for its own sake.

Convey that you are connected to people by using common literary reference points. Great speakers often use fiction—including film and biography—to inspire their audiences. We can all relate to the hilarious line, "I'll have what she's having!" from the film *When Harry Met Sally . . .*, but can you use this quote to segue to a serious point? If you speak to people in recovery, you might quote screenwriter Nora Ephron, "Above all, be the heroine of your life, not the victim." A beloved Shakespearean tale like *The Tempest* can be a metaphor for local politics. Whatever you choose, people will relax when you open with, "I'd like to tell you a story . . ."

You want to speak *with* people as if in a conversation, not *at* them.

Speak about Controversy As an Outsider Would

Most women are outside "the establishment" of powerbrokers and top decision-makers. Women speakers will gain their audience's attention if they are bold and willing to attack questionable decisions made by today's leaders. As outsiders, women can question the establishment and challenge the status quo, even with regard to U.S. economic policy, a daunting topic for most of us. However, as the blog *She-conomy.com* points out, women control the consumer economy, accounting for 85 percent of all consumer purchases including everything from autos to health care. Women purchase 91 percent of new homes, 66 percent of all PCs, pay for 92 percent of vacations, 80 percent of health-care expenses, 65 percent of new cars; women own 89 percent of all bank accounts, purchase 93 percent of food sold, and purchase 93 percent of over-the-counter pharmaceuticals. Let us agree that women understand the value of a dollar.

Women speakers can use a "kitchen table economics" approach to explaining complex and suspicious mortgage practices such as "robo-signing" in everyday language and a conversational tone that people appreciate. When you masterfully present financial material, you are confronting the stereotype that *girls are innately bad at math*. Run the numbers, predict the cash flow, and make transparent to the average worker what the percentages and ratios really mean.

As women, we need to reach for leadership roles across every sector by speaking up in public venues. Americans are cynical about present-day leaders, who are mostly male. Distrust is in the air. Yours will be the fresh face. There is no doubt that society will benefit when twice as many people apply their brainpower to attacking today's complex dilemmas. At the podium, women can emphasize that they have not created the urgent problems of the day but do have new ideas for solving them. When more women feel empowered at the podium, their collective voices will create what author Gregg Easterbrook has called a "sonic boom"; and sonic booms can shatter glass ceilings. Knowing that, let your voice be heard.

Power Up! Three Ways to Build Credibility and Make Yourself Heard

by Claire Damken Brown, PhD
Founder and president of
Damken Brown and Associates, Inc.

"If women are seen and not heard, they lose the opportunity to contribute their ideas and be evaluated equitably for that next promotion."

Are there challenging issues affecting women's careers that still need to be addressed? Yes. Several challenges still confront women on their journey to that CEO office in the sky. Challenges include:

- Lack of workplace support: lackadaisical and ineffective leadership programs and career sponsors for women.
- Stereotypes (yes—unbelievable—but those stereotypes are still out there): Can a woman raise a family, be a nuclear physicist, and prepare the tuna casserole all at the same time? And:
- Differences in the value placed on men's and women's communication behaviors that make women appear less capable and credible.

Some businesses are seriously working on mentoring and leadership programs for women and creating an inclusive work environment. Yet it is difficult to form a systemic change that would erase these challenges altogether. One communication issue that continues to plague working women is that of not being heard and, therefore, feeling invisible. Especially in male-dominated work environments, women frequently lament that their ideas are not as respected, their opinions are not as valued, their voices are often silenced, and they are more frequently interrupted when compared to similar behaviors of their male colleagues. If women can't get their voices heard or have their comments taken seriously, then they can't build on-the-job credibility; without that credibility women cannot be accurately evaluated for promotions and career opportunities that will propel them to the executive suite.

Some may argue that women are now occupying more managerial roles, getting those promotions to upper-level jobs, and being selected for the CEO role (note the promotion of Ms. Marissa Mayer to the CEO role at Yahoo! Inc.). However in the midst of Mayer's promotion accolades, there was much discussion about her being six months pregnant and her plans to return to work after a two-week maternity leave, rather than discussions focusing on the expertise she brought to the CEO position. When she did take a two-week maternity leave when her son was born, the debate centered on whether or not "she could both lead the embattled Internet giant and be a good mother." Statistics from Catalyst, an organization that advocates for working women, show that in 2012 women in the *Fortune* 500 companies comprised 4.2 percent of the CEOs, 16.6 percent of board seats, 14.3 percent of executive officers, and 8.1 percent of the top earners.

What is a woman to do?

Women *can* learn specific communication behaviors to increase their impact and workplace credibility.

Let us look at three communication behaviors that differ between men and women and influence credibility:

1. Managing interruptions (how to keep or take back the floor)
2. Exercising the art of the brief response (or, when to stop talking)
3. Preventing idea theft (for instance, when he shares an amazing idea . . . the same one she said ten minutes earlier)

By gaining insight into men's and women's communication styles, women learn communication choices they can use to be certain their messages get heard. Controlling these three communication behaviors is a crucial first step toward increasing women's voices and credibility. After all, if women are seen and not heard, they lose the opportunity to contribute their ideas and be evaluated equitably for that next promotion.

Managing Interruptions: "As I Was Saying . . ."

Many folks think women talk more than men do. However, when in groups of men and women, for instance a business meeting, men actually talk more than women and hold the floor for a longer time than women. Men interrupt women more than women interrupt men. These behaviors result in women not getting their thoughts, ideas, and opinions heard! If a woman is viewed as not speaking up, then there might be a tendency to view her as uninterested, not knowledgeable, not a team player, or not wanting that promotion.

Interruptions can be viewed as supportive: "Hey, great idea," "I agree," or simply, "uh-huh." On the other hand, they can be viewed as dismissive or challenging, and the subject will be changed: "You're off base," "We should talk about this first . . ." or "That's not important." Research by Candace West on power, status, and gender in doctor-patient encounters has shown that women tend to use more supportive interruptions than men do, aimed at encouraging the speaker by verbalizing agreement or acknowledgement while the speaker is talking. It is not aimed at taking power away from the speaker or establishing dominance. Other writers about gendered communications (including Julia Wood, Teri Kwai Gamble, Michael Gamble, and Deborah Tannen) note that men tend to use more disruptive interruptions such as actively changing the subject, controlling the conversation, and taking the floor away from the speaker. Interrupted women leave the meeting thinking the men are rude and do not listen; the women may feel frustrated at not fully expressing themselves. The men leave thinking the women just were not up to the challenge; they feel confident that they got their ideas out there.

Once interrupted, to gain control back, my coauthor, Audrey Nelson, and I have given numerous suggestions in our book *Code Switching: How to Talk So Men Will Listen*. A woman can use the following phrases: "Just a second," "I'm not quite done yet," "I'll be with you in a moment," "One minute while I finish," "Thanks for that insight, I'll finish now," "I'll continue now without interruptions," or "Hold that thought"—see similar suggestions by Phyllis Mindell. My coauthor and I also suggested in *The Gender Communication Handbook: Conquering Conversational Collisions Between Men and Women,* that a woman can directly look at the interrupter, establish momentary eye contact, and "make a statement, using the person's name if she knows it: 'Bryan, I'll take comments in a moment.'" She then continues talking to the group and completes her ideas. She may reestablish her dominance as speaker by leaning forward in the direction of the interrupter, speaking louder, and if seated, standing up to draw attention back to her. Be prepared to manage these interruptions at meetings. Use these techniques to get your own voice heard, or as a facilitator, use them to insure the other women at the meeting are heard.

Exercising the Art of the Brief Response: When One Is Plenty

Women's communication style is relational; it is aimed at building and maintaining relationships. Their talk patterns are indirect and process- and other-oriented—discussing family, friends, emotions, feelings, details, and personal issues. Men's communication style is task oriented and competitive; its focus is to exchange information and data. Men's talk patterns are direct and self-oriented—discussing jobs, work goals, business, sports, finances, winning, and completion dates. Women tend to collaborate and share thoughts and ideas. Men tend to compete and challenge each other with their banter, outdoing each other, and establishing dominance.

When a man asks a woman a question, he generally is not expecting all her story's details: who said what to whom, what she was wearing, what the waiter spilled at the lunch meeting, etc. About now, he is checking his watch wondering why he even asked the question. Men may view her long detailed story as an indicator that she is not focused, does not know, or is making excuses. He wants that bottom line: short, sweet, and direct. She wants to tell the details because that sharing makes it a memorable and informative story supporting their relationship.

Remember that the men are expecting a direct short response; my coauthor and I offered the following remedy in *Code Switching*. Think: "one is plenty." Answer with one word: yes, no, or maybe. If he needs more information, he will ask. Then she can answer with one sentence. If he still needs more information or a clarification, he will ask. She can respond with one paragraph.

One word. One sentence. One paragraph. That is it. One is plenty.

For example, a man asks, "Will you talk with the customer on Thursday?"

She says, "No." (One word.)

He asks, "When will you talk with that customer?"

She replies, "Probably early Friday, if I get all the data on time from Bob." (One sentence.)

Wanting more information he asks, "Are there issues with Bob's work that I should know about?"

She states, "Bob has been sick and out of the office for a few days. He has the data, but I was not able to contact him. He is back now, and we have talked a few times. He will get his data to me Thursday, and I will add it to the report and talk with the customer Friday. I will set up a conference call today for Friday morning." (One paragraph.)

Alternatively, she can ask him for clarification: "Is this a yes or no question, or do you want the details?" Women, use these suggestions to take charge and manage how you respond to men's questions.

Preventing Idea Theft:
Proactive Approaches

Ever been in a meeting, stated an idea that seems to be ignored, then ten minutes later a man says the same thing and everyone responds, "Great idea, Frank"? Then the group discusses the idea for another ten minutes giving Frank full credit, remarking how wonderful Frank's idea was, and how it is going to make the company big bucks. I think this has happened to every woman I know. It is as if she is invisible. No one heard her. Yet, when Frank says the same thing, it is fantastic. How can women prevent or manage this idea theft and get the credit they deserve?

Knowing that there is a possibility their ideas may not be heard, women can do several things to prepare for the meeting, as suggested in my coauthored book, *Code Switching*. Many meetings are scheduled in advance. Once she knows the topic, she can write down her ideas and bring paper copies to the meeting. Alternatively, she can e-mail the meeting attendees a day before the meeting providing her ideas for discussion at tomorrow's meeting. At the meeting itself, she states her idea. If her idea seems to be ignored and then gets repeated by another, she needs to draw the attention back to herself and her idea. For example she could say, "Frank, glad you think my idea will work. Let me give the group a few more data points."

Remember when you were in grade school and went on outings? Each student had a buddy to hold hands, keep track of each other, and help when needed. Get a buddy! Ask your buddy (woman or man) to support your ideas at the meeting. When Allison mentions an idea, her buddy might say, "Tell us more about that." If someone repeats her idea later in the meeting, her buddy could state, "That is what Allison was talking about a few minutes ago. Allison, why don't you explain how it will work?" The buddy system works well, too, for managing interruptions. Have that same buddy use one of the phrases listed earlier for managing interruptions. "Hold that thought. Let's let Allison finish her idea."

Do not let yourselves be silenced. Women, it is time to power up! Be ready. Take charge of the conversation. Use these tools to be heard and build the credibility you deserve!

Eight Key Ways Women Become Natural and Necessary Leaders

by Lois P. Frankel, PhD
President of Corporate Coaching International

"If ever there was a time in history that cried out for women to lead, that time is now."

For centuries, women have unwittingly honed the quintessential qualities that are necessary for successful leadership. Whether acquired through nature or nurture, women are adept in building relationships, encouraging and motivating others to succeed, carefully crafting their communications, and creating environments of trust and safety. These represent but a few of the behaviors that qualify them as outstanding leaders. Despite the fact that women lead all the time, they are not so bold as to call themselves leaders. Many have learned the hard way that when a woman steps up to lead she is demeaned, ridiculed, and worse.

Yet as we look around the world and see economic decline, famine, poverty, corporate greed, and war—created and perpetuated by predominantly male leadership—it is clear that if ever there was a time in history that cried out for women to lead, that time is now. It is not that women make better leaders.

It is that women make *different* leaders. We know from history that to be successful, *you must be a leader for your time*. For Great Britain, 1979 was the year for Margaret Thatcher's unique brand of leadership. The time had come in 2008 for Barack Obama to be elected the first African-American leader of the free world. Now, the time has come for women to step up confidently and courageously to the leadership plate.

The truth is, what followers expect from leaders in the first decades of the 21st century—and perhaps beyond—are the behaviors and characteristics that women have traditionally been socialized to exhibit. Command and control leadership is dead. We live in an age of cooperation and collaboration. A time when the carrot is more powerful than the stick. In short, a time well suited for a woman's unique brand of leadership. It does not mean that men cannot or do not display these qualities but rather that women tend to do so with greater ease, confidence, and comfort.

The changing face of leadership is threatening to men because it requires thinking in a way that is counter to their own socialization and, in some cases, education. Similarly, women may feel threatened because it asks them to begin assuming responsibility in ways they may never before have considered and to call attention to skills they have been admonished to hide.

Nice girls (women who behave according to the messages they received in childhood for how little girls should act) have a particularly difficult time assuming leadership roles and doing it effectively. When they do, they often try to make everyone happy (which is impossible), delay decision-making by trying to get *everyone's* buy-in, hesitate to take necessary risks for fear of offending the powers that be, and communicate in ways that undermine their confidence and credibility. Ironically, each of these behaviors could work to the advantage of women—if only they would balance them with new behaviors that contribute to more effective leadership. In other words, stepping fully away from the nice girl messages learned in childhood, and into adulthood, is all it would take for *any* woman to be a phenomenal leader for this age.

This essay illuminates eight key ways you can enhance, hone, and apply your leadership talents to make your voice heard and influence others when critical decisions are made that impact your company, your community, your family, and the world.

Sit at the Table

As I wrote in 2006, this statement is meant literally and figuratively. When entering a crowded meeting room, avoid the temptation to sit on the periphery so that "more important" people can sit at the table. Even if it means pulling a chair up to squeeze yourself in, do it. If you are not literally sitting at the table, your voice will not count. Once at the table, speak early and often. Early speakers are seen as more self-confident than later speakers are. If you do not have an opinion about the topic at hand, you can still have your voice heard by asking a question, answering a question, or supporting what someone else has proposed. In your own home, sit at the head of the dinner table regardless of how many men are present. You *earned* that place.

Get to the Point

Women make the mistake of using far more words than necessary or effective. We do it to fill in silences, because we think it is only fair to share everything in our heads, and because we mistakenly believe that more words will make us sound more authoritative. Wrong, wrong, and wrong.

Fewer words strengthen a message, but more words soften it.

Before saying anything, think first about the most important thing that you want others to take away from your communication. Then say this in one sentence, followed by two or three pieces of supporting data. If you have a difficult time knowing when to stop talking, try adding the tagline, "Do you have any questions about what I just said?" as a way to toss the ball into the other person's court and elicit discussion.

Get in the Risk Game

If you are one of those people who always plays it safe, you have to exercise your risk muscle. You can do this by taking small personal risks and learning that the results are rarely catastrophic.

The next time someone asks for your opinion, and you know it's contrary to that person's viewpoint, take the risk of putting

your perspective on the table rather than taking the path of least resistance by agreeing or saying you have no opinion.

When you are in a meeting with people who tend to be more verbal than you are, take the risk of jumping into the debate rather than waiting for just the right moment. When your mother-in-law tells you she is coming for a month in January (when two weeks is about all anyone in the family can bear), let her know you are delighted she is coming and that two weeks would work best for the family. There are plenty of ways you can gradually expand your self-imposed comfort zone.

Think Strategically, but Act Tactically

Before rolling up your sleeves and jumping into an assignment, ask yourself strategic questions such as, "Is this the right thing to be doing? Will doing this add value? What is the most efficient way to do it? Should I be doing this or is someone else better suited? What might be a better idea that would make us more competitive?" Once you have answered these questions (either alone or with your team), then develop the tactics that will achieve the ultimately agreed upon goal or direction. Women actually do this quite naturally. How else can they get three kids to three different events on a Saturday, pick up the laundry, visit a sick friend, and prepare dinner for guests? We just do not call it strategic and tactical.

Resist Perfectionism

We have all heard the saying, "a woman has to work twice as hard to be considered half as good." Do not let it guide your actions. Thinking that you have to be perfect constricts your strategic thinking and willingness to take risks. The balance of strategic thinking and tactical implementation is by nature imperfect—and always a risk. The most important thing to remember is that if you do make a mistake, people just want you to acknowledge it, assess what you have learned from it, and say it will not happen again. While you are at it, skip the apology. A simple statement of fact about what went wrong should take its place. This holds true at home as much as it does at work. Abandon the notion that you can be the perfect mother, employee, daughter, and friend—it is an exercise in futility.

Volunteer to Make Formal and Informal Presentations

People often tell me I am a great public speaker. I am always flattered by the feedback, but the fact of the matter is I am simply practiced. From the time I was president of my high school junior and senior classes, I have been in front of a microphone. When circumstances keep me from speaking for any length of time, I am as anxious as the next person when I have to walk up to the podium and begin a presentation. If you want to become really good at influencing others, seize every opportunity to go outside your comfort zone and speak before large and small groups. Also, consider joining Toastmasters International as a means of honing your oratory skills.

Solicit 360-Degree Feedback

There really is no better way than feedback to have the mirror held up so you can see yourself as others see you. Getting feedback is akin to a focus group conducted for the purpose of improving a brand. Making three simple requests will yield a wealth of information—usually about behaviors related to emotional intelligence: Tell me two or three things I do well and should continue doing. Tell me two or three things I can do more of to be even more effective. Tell me two or three things I can do less of to be even more effective. As with any kind of feedback or survey, be prepared to take action. We have a saying in coaching, *"If three people say you're drunk, lie down."*

Consciously Build Your Leadership Brand

We are all brands in the workplace. People talk about us the same as they might a movie, a washing machine, or a car. They have opinions about us and are usually willing to share them with anyone who asks. It is your responsibility to construct the message that you want others to communicate about you. Start by writing down what you want people to say about you when you leave a room. Fill in the blank, "She's a leader who _____." Be as specific as possible. Include what you want to do, how you want to do it, and what people will get out of doing it with you. Then identify the actions in which you must engage if you are to make that statement a reality. For example, if you want others to say, "She's a leader who exhibits courage," then take risks around saying things others are thinking but will not say. Be willing to go out on a limb for a new idea that could potentially yield great rewards but isn't a slam dunk, or implement new policies that might not immediately be popular but that will make your company more competitive.

Although I have provided eight coaching tips here, you do not have to implement all of them to become the leader you were destined to be. What you will find is changing just two or three behaviors will automatically create dramatic shifts in how you feel about yourself, how others perceive you, and the impact that you make. The rest will come naturally.

Soft Is the New Hard: The Hidden Power of Feminine Skills

by Birute Regine, EdD
Founder of Iron Butterfly Power Circles

"By employing feminine skills women are redefining the use of power and the meaning of leadership."

I was interviewing Kim Campbell, former prime minister of Canada, for my book *Iron Butterflies: Women Transforming Themselves and the World*. We sat in her office at Harvard's Kennedy School of Government, where she was teaching at the time. As we chatted, she told me about a time when she was the Minister of Justice in Canada and was given the difficult task of getting a piece of legislation on gun control passed, which at the time was still a contentious issue.

Under her stewardship the gun control bill passed by a very large majority and produced no enemies, a huge feat. Not unreasonably, Kim expected to have a few accolades thrown her way. Instead of hearing the press praise her for achieving what she promised—for getting the bill through—here was the media's reaction: "How did it possibly go through? She must have watered it down." Kim was baffled; why was she not getting credit for navigating a difficult legislative path and accomplishing what she had promised?

When I asked what she did to get the piece of legislation through she told me her strategy. Kim would get dissenting sides together, those who usually didn't talk to each another. She needed to know when to push and when to pull in, strategically moving people toward agreement. She recognized that it would take an enormous amount of consultation, usually behind the scenes, and she knew it would require lots of careful handling. Even when Kim had the votes she needed simply to pass the legislation, she felt it was not enough. It was important to her to keep the solidarity of her own party, but also to negotiate the dissent. She achieved that extra goal.

Many of the behaviors she spoke of that contributed to her eventual success were what I call feminine skills: inclusion, relational intelligence, deep listening, empathy, intuition, big picture thinking, finding the common ground, and bridge building. These, however, are not the skills we usually associate with "leadership." The media did not actually *see* Kim's leadership because they were looking for other kinds of behaviors, which they associate with strong leadership.

If you think about it, our image of leadership is masculine infused. Our society rewards these masculine skills: being independent, strategic, linear, decisive, and goal-directed—the Lone Ranger style of leadership. This is what we often think of as being a strong leader. Of course, these are important skills to have as a leader. Kim had these skills as well.

However, she also had more; she had feminine skills. Having both feminine and masculine skills at her disposal made her very resourceful. However, the skills that proved to be the most effective in this situation for developing a cooperative spirit were her feminine skills. Since she did not trumpet her accomplishments and did not make all kinds of noises and declarations, the media did not recognize her leadership. They were looking for more masculine behavior and did not see it; Kim was not a leader. There was a total disconnect between her manner of dealing with a difficult piece of legislation and the success she had with it. They did not see the power of feminine skills for achieving her goal.

It's not just women who are invisible in this leadership style. Male leaders who work to create more collaborative workplaces, including tending to relationships, are often as invisible in their leadership skills as women because people don't associate these skills with being a powerful leader. Men who embrace more feminine skills in their leadership style are often criticized as being weak. Regardless of what you think of the politics of President Obama, he is someone who has been criticized for not being a strong enough leader because he doesn't try to dominate, to show his muscle. He doesn't use his power to dominate, which is what we think of as being strong; he uses his power to try to collaborate.

Historically, in politics and business, feminine skills have been largely disparaged, demeaned, and marginalized, as touchy-feely, as soft. Nevertheless, in reality, they are anything but soft; they are the exact opposite. These skills are *hard* to learn; they are difficult and complex skills to acquire and develop. You cannot learn relational intelligence in a two-hour seminar. Soft is the new hard, the exact opposite of what we have been led to believe.

Feminine skills are also *powerful* skills to have in our interconnected, interdependent global world, and now there is a science that explains why: complexity science. Complexity science explores the world of complex adaptive systems. A key feature of complex systems is emergence. University of Michigan physicist John Holland, one of the founders of complexity science, once described emergence as "much coming from little," which makes it sound almost magical. Most people would use a more prosaic phrase, "The whole is greater than the sum of the parts."

Here is the equation: what emerges from a complex system is determined principally by how agents in a system interact with each other. The quality of those interactions has everything to do with what properties emerge in the system. Families, organizations, communities are complex systems. When we translate that complexity equation into human terms, agents are *people* and the interactions are *relationships*. We can now say that how people relate to one another has everything to do with what emerges in an organization. What emerges reveals the organization's culture, creativity, innovation, and productivity. If you want to have a positive, constructive culture, then attend to creating positive, open, and trusting relationships.

How do we create strong and positive relationships? By employing our feminine skills. Skills such as relational intelligence, emotional intelligence, inclusion, and empathy serve to strengthen our relationships.

Furthermore, complex systems that have strong positive connections are more resilient, adaptable, and robust. In organizations, positive, strong relationships contribute to the organization's resilience because an organization that has a strong sense of community will be more adaptable and robust, all necessary attributes to have in our fast-changing times. Who would have thought that a human-centered strategy for business success and personal fulfillment would flow from a short but powerful equation of complexity science? However, it does.

Feminine skills are also powerful because these skills are needed to develop true collaborations. Given the complexity of issues we face today we need people working together to solve them. Recent research shows that a collaborative group can perform at a level of creativity that is higher than that of any single individual.

Social scientists, such as Christopher Chabris at MIT's Center for Collective Intelligence and Anita Williams Woolley at Carnegie Mellon University, have recently begun to systematically examine what they call the "collective intelligence" of groups. Collective intelligence is a measure of how smart the group is, as a whole, as reported in a paper by Woolley and Chabris, "Evidence for a Collective Intelligence Factor in the Performance of Human Groups." The study attracted interest in the national business press.

What they discovered in their research completely surprised them; it was not something they expected, nor were they looking for it. They learned that collective intelligence is not tied to either the smartest person on the team or to the average intelligence of the members of the team.

Rather it is something that is greater than any individual contribution or the sum of contributions. It is an emergent property that results from the interactions among the people in the group. What emerges is almost magical: something greater than the sum of its parts. You can call it "evolved thinking."

Complexity science shows us that for a positive emergence to occur in complex systems there must be conditions of mutuality and a level playing field, diversity, and trust. If these are not present, the potential for collective intelligence can easily devolve into group think, where everyone dumbly follows the boss's lead.

The current research on collective intelligence gives us two key results. The first is that the phenomenon is real, that groups can indeed perform at a higher level of creativity than any single individual. We knew this intuitively, of course. It is the second result that is the surprise, and this has to do with the one single predictor that a particular group will have high collective intelligence: at least half the chairs around the table should be occupied by women.

What do women bring to the table that catalyzes evolved thinking? According to Chabris and Woolley it is a superior social sensitivity in reading nonverbal cues and other people's emotions, and a fairness in turn taking. Here again, it is the power of feminine skills, skills that facilitate the emergence of collective intelligence.

Feminine skills are powerful because they influence what kind of culture emerges in an organization. They contribute to the overall robustness, adaptability, and resilience of an organization, and they facilitate the emergence of collective intelligence.

These feminine skills can in part explain why women have such a positive effect on businesses. In the 2010 report "Invest in Women, Invest in America: A Comprehensive Review of Women in the U.S. Economy," the U.S. Congress Joint Economic Committee reported that companies with a significant block of women on their boards of directors tend to outperform those with few women at the helm, boasting 65 percent higher returns on invested capital, 54 percent higher return on equity, and 42 percent higher return on sales. The twenty-five *Fortune* 500 companies with the best records for promoting women to senior positions have 69 percent higher returns than the *Fortune* 500 median for their industry.

The results of the McKinsey Global Survey in 2010 "Moving Women to the Top" found 72 percent of executives believe there is a direct connection between a company's gender diversity and its financial success. The study showed that the companies with the highest levels of gender diversity also had higher returns on equity, operating results, and growth in market valuation than the averages in their respective sectors.

So-called feminine skills are not exclusively held by women, of course. But on average they are more developed in women, and women are generally more willing to use them. And certainly these skills need to be developed, recognized, and appreciated in both the men and women who employ them.

Know that feminine skills are not "soft." They are hard and powerful skills to have in our interconnected world. Be clear about the skills you have to offer and value them. If you are a connector, who likes to bring people together, or an effective bridge builder between different perspectives, or a facilitator able to bring difficult people along, know that these are skills that define the new kind of leadership, a more collaborative, interactive leadership.

Let's not take these skills for granted or overlook them. Let's begin to acknowledge, appreciate, and reward the people who employ these skills.

When we embrace the power of our feminine skills, we are redefining leadership where the feminine is as strong and powerful as the masculine. We are transforming the meaning of power: from power *over others* to power *used for and with others*.

A profound social transformation is underway that holds the potential to create a more collaborative world, replacing an ultimately unsustainable world of domination. As women are beginning to gain access to the power tables, the skills that were marginalized and demeaned by the patriarchal system as "touchy-feely" are now the very skills that empower them to create a better world, to lead in a new era. Embrace your feminine skills. Embrace your place as a leader.

Part Two

Mastering Our Internal Environment

Did you like those wonderful techniques in the first section? You can readily learn those techniques and skills to increase your influence in the external world. Just remember to share your learning and success with other women. If each one teaches one, we can do anything.

Nevertheless, no matter how much success we meet in the outside world, we will not feel fulfilled unless we build a solid internal foundation. In this second section, nine essays address the internal barriers that too often prevent women from wielding their power and enjoying satisfying, productive lives. The stories in this section focus on techniques for engaging our minds and hearts to understand and acknowledge that we can indeed improve the world.

These essays all offer different insights on ways to create congruency between our self-image and our sense of place in the world. Creating a match between the two can powerfully affect our ability to claim empowerment and achieve our goals. Which stories resonate with you? Open your heart and mind to the stories in this section, watch your self-inflicted barriers dissolve, and fill your life with love and joy.

Do You Need a Reason to Love?

by Marci Shimoff
Author of the *New York Times* bestsellers
Love for No Reason and *Happy for No Reason*

"When you fill your own love tank,
you bring that love to everything in your life."

The woman sitting across from me was radiant. Mirabai Devi, an international spiritual teacher from South Africa, was known for the unconditional love that emanated from her, and I could see why. Her dark eyes sparkled, her smile was both serene and joyful, and I felt a warm glow in my heart as I gazed at her.

I pressed the Record button on my digital recorder, and Mirabai began to tell me about her first experience of unconditional love. It had taken place almost twenty years earlier, when, as a young woman, Mirabai experienced an awakening while traveling through Europe:

"It was as if a dam burst in my heart, and the waters overflowed. The love that came forth was unlike anything I had ever experienced before. Like a flood, it was all-consuming and all-encompassing; I could hardly contain it. I felt electrified; my body was tingling all over. I was so in love with the whole creation that I wanted to hug everyone I met. I knew that I could not do that because people would think I was crazy. Still, people could feel it. Everywhere I went they would just come up to me and say, 'What can I do for you?' 'Can I help you?' 'Can I give you a ride?' 'Can I get you some food?' 'Can I . . . ?' They just wanted to be around me.

"Traveling through Holland one afternoon, I stopped on the side of the road and looked at a field of cabbages. All the cabbages were just filled with this iridescent, luminous light. My heart was bursting with love for the cabbages.

"I felt union with the whole of creation. Everything was pulsing with love.

"It was in the walls and in the trees. It was as though it was coming through the sky. I saw that everything is connected and everything is one. And everything is radiant with this exquisite, ecstatic love."

I sat transfixed, taking in the details of Mirabai's remarkable story, and asking myself: Is it possible for me and for others to experience that state of unconditional love all the time?

That was the question I set out to answer in my latest book, *Love for No Reason: 7 Steps to Creating a Life of Unconditional Love*. Taking the same approach I had in my earlier book, *Happy for No Reason*, in which I interviewed unconditionally happy people to find out how to be truly happy, I went to the experts on love. I spoke to more than 150 people I call "Love Luminaries," including scientists, psychologists, spiritual teachers, and people whose lives were rich in the qualities of the heart—to find out how to be unconditionally loving.

In interview after interview, I heard more than a hundred variations of Mirabai's story. I thought, "If so many people, from all different backgrounds and all different walks of life experience this, it must be possible for me, and anyone else."

What I discovered through my research is that each of us can grow in unconditional love, the kind of love that does not depend on any person or situation, what I call Love for No Reason. I found fourteen keys that will help you experience this higher state of love more and more of the time. Here are three tips to get you started:

1. Anchor Yourself in Safety

Feeling unsafe or fearful essentially takes love offline. It is impossible to activate the physiology of unconditional love when your body is in fight or flight.

One way to relieve the stress response and establish a feeling of inner safety is to mentally take stock of your circles of support: physical, emotional, and spiritual. Review the resources inside and around you that you can draw on to deal with whatever life throws at you—your family and friends, your talents, your faith, your work, your hobbies; whatever and whomever you love and feel strengthened by. Spend at least one full minute savoring each circle of support. Let your mind and body consciously experience the feeling of being supported and safe. When you register and savor the experience of safety, it creates new neural pathways in your brain.

2. Feel Your Feelings

Stifling your emotions or expressing them excessively is equally damaging to your capacity to experience unconditional love. Luckily, there is a third option: feeling your feelings. This is not the same as "expressing, exaggerating, or acting out"; as Love Luminary Raphael Cushnir told me, "All it requires is a gentle focus, a turning toward what's actually present."

Try this simple practice to help maintain openness that I adapted from Raphael's work. To begin, think of a negative feeling that you resist (such as anger, jealousy, sadness, or fear). Next, recall how you feel standing in a hot shower—the stream of hot water cascading over your body. Use your felt memory to actually re-create the expansion, relaxation, and openness of that experience in your body. Now, bring this same sense of bodily relaxation to feel that negative feeling you resist. Notice how your body relaxes and expands, and in that bigger space, the stuck feeling can now start to move. When you remove the interference to the flow of emotions, like leaves on a river they stay with you briefly and soon move round the bend. Then you are free to experience the underlying Love for No Reason that is present all the time.

3. Practice Self-Compassion

Try a simple self-love technique that brings you into your heart and reminds you to treat yourself with care. It comes in especially handy whenever you are having a rough time or being critical toward yourself or others. Throughout the day, ask yourself, "What's the most loving thing I can do for myself right now?" or "What's the most loving way I can be with myself right now?" Then pay attention to the answer and actually do whatever it is.

Sometimes it is having compassion for the part of you that is hurting; other times it is forgiving yourself for mistakes or simply lightening up on yourself. There are also occasions when the most loving thing you can do for yourself is taking a walk or a hot bath or calling a good friend for a chat. Whatever it is, when you love and take care of yourself, you will find it inevitably serves everyone.

Practice these simple exercises frequently and you will notice more love in your heart.

Learning to experience pure love within yourself is the key to living a life of unconditional love.

When you fill your own love tank, you bring that love to everything in your life. Then, as Mirabai experienced, you still love people and things outside yourself, but the difference is that your love doesn't depend on any of those things, whether people, jobs, relationships, cars, clothes—or even cabbages.

Poise, the Final Ingredient

by Linda Rendleman
Cofounder of the Women Like Us Foundation

*"To be authentic you need to understand
your values and live by them."*

I love this word, poise. It is usually defined as dignity, ease of manner, composure, and calm, but it makes me think of other words like grace, peace, compassion, wisdom, purpose, and authenticity. Many poised women I have been fortunate to meet have a gift for moving through life with a certain grace and compassion, for letting go of anger, ignoring pettiness, and living graciously and with faith. Sometimes it feels like they have a secret. In addition, somewhere in that secret place they understand who they are and who that little girl inside is; the one who grew up to be this complete person.

Poise is certainly a final ingredient for creating change and illuminating the lives of others.

Poise Is Wisdom

Poise reflects wisdom, an acceptance that things do not happen overnight and that there are certain things we cannot transform.

The knowledge that life is not always fair and it's nobody's fault. Poise is an understanding that putting one foot in front of the other is part of the power we have as human beings, as women. It is realizing that we do our part to make a difference in the world through patience, commitment, and endurance. It is also knowing that putting our wisdom to use is one of the greatest gifts we can give to others and ourselves.

I have marveled at women that I have known who demonstrate poise by taking responsibility for the direction of their own lives through their strength and perseverance. They understand their challenges and focus their lives toward their goals, no matter the barriers. They are anchored into what is true for them. They have evolved beyond the obstacles of the everyday, have become present with their own passions and purpose, and have acted on them for a better future.

Are you choosing to respond to the world with compassion and giving? Are you choosing to use your resources of patience, tenacity, wisdom, and compassion to realize your gifts? Are you living with poise?

Some women embody poise, such as Audrey Hepburn did. She not only carried herself beautifully in a physical way, but also in her speech, her manner, and her sense of being. Audrey was unassuming and reserved about her celebrity status. However, she knew what to do with it when the time came to make an impact. She was quick to speak out for the children she met, for those in need who otherwise had no voice.

As a child, she lived in war-torn Holland during World War II. She continually marveled at how her life ended up the way it did. She had said, "My career is a complete mystery to me. It has been a total surprise since the first day. I never set out to be an actress." Yet, all admired her magnetism and her spirit, and she is one of the most renowned actresses of our time.

It was through her poise, her courage, her compassion, and her grace that Audrey was able to set an example to all while caring for others. She always considered her work as an ambassador with UNICEF as her greatest role.

Poise Is Understanding

I am a member of a speakers' website. Through it, I can promote myself as a speaker and author, and offer my services to anyone who may want to hire a motivational speaker for a female audience for an event or meeting. This website offers the public a link to contact the speakers for more information.

I had not accessed the site for a long time when one day I had some time and thought I would browse it again. I realized I had never checked the messages page. There it was, a two-year-old e-mail from a man by the name of Roger, asking if I was the same Linda Rendleman who went to elementary school in Morrison, Illinois, in 1957.

The answer was a definite yes. However, I did not remember Roger. My curiosity piqued, I e-mailed back, never really expecting that Roger would even still be available at that address. After a short wait, he responded.

Roger was trying to find me because his parents had passed away and as he was clearing out their home, he found a black and white photo he had taken of me, little eight-year-old Linda Rendleman, standing on the sidewalk in the middle of winter in 1957. He said he would send the picture to me.

When I received that never before seen picture of this little girl, I cried. Was I crying for the little girl who is no longer? Was I crying for the little girl who looked so sad, standing on that sidewalk in the gray of winter dressed in the dark red poodle coat with a headscarf tied neatly under her chin? She was not smiling. Her eyes looked sad and pierced through me. I wanted to know her better. I wondered where she went. I did not feel like I knew that little girl any longer because through my fears, my many moves as a child, my attendance at fifteen schools in the span of fourteen years, I had hidden her away. She could not be sad or scared. She had to be strong, to be tough, to belong, to be accepted. Therefore, she held back the fearful, sensitive little girl inside of her and came out as a self-sufficient, "I can do anything" woman-warrior.

Seeing my childhood picture from fifty years earlier truly was the first time I met and confronted my inner young self. Not once during occasional therapy, nor in educational courses to become a counselor, had I realized the impact that my childhood had on my future.

Since that picture came my way, I have had a greater understanding of that person inside of me, the one who as a child looked at the world with wonder, striving to find her place and be a part of it. I understand that girl who was sensitive, who loved to be loved, and wanted to be a gift to the world in a special way; the girl, then the yearning young woman, then the grown woman who seeks wisdom each and every day.

The complexities of my life experiences have affected how I have chosen to respond to what comes my way. I have gained wisdom. I have become authentic. I pray I am growing into the woman who reflects poise.

How do you acquire poise, you ask? How do you find your authentic self? Perhaps you already have, but here are some of my ideas:

- Poise comes when we recognize lessons from our experiences and understand the importance of acceptance and growth from them.
- Poise comes from a certain peaceful core you develop out of your experiential knowledge and intentions for understanding meaning and challenge in this world. Many cultures revere the aged for the knowledge they can impart from their experiences. This is a beautiful way to understand and embrace the process of aging, to be sure.
- Poise can be developed at any age. Your own brand of poise can change over the years when you integrate the struggles and experiences, celebrations and joys you have had along the way. It's a committed, inner knowing that the duty of women—including women like us—is to stand up to the world, graciously continuing with our message of connectivity and support of mankind and keeping alive our determination to enrich our lives as well as the lives of others.

Poise Is Being Authentic

If you want to carry yourself with poise, you must understand who you are—who you *really* are. Take a look at your accomplishments when you were a child. What experiences did you have; what goals did you achieve that are part of who you are today? What values are important to you? To be authentic you need to understand your values and live by them.

There is a simple exercise you can do to get clear. Here is how it goes. Make a long list using single words to signify all the things that are important to you. Use words like honesty, trustworthiness, partnership, creativity, and excellence. Try to come up with at least twenty-five of them. Then pick the top three—only three. Once you have selected the top three, write a mission statement that includes them.

For example, I selected self-expression, love, and zest. My mission statement goes like this: My purpose is to give myself the freedom to creatively express myself, spread love to all I come in contact with, and demonstrate an enthusiasm in all that I do.

Now do it again. Pick the next three values and create another mission statement. Then create a third mission statement. What you will learn is what really matters to you. When you understand what your values truly are, you are on your way to living your own authentic life. The only thing left is to remind yourself of your values every day, as you commit yourself to staying on track.

When you were working on the exercises and claiming your true values, you were working on your own brand of poise, on creating and being true to your authentic self.

Finally, Poise Is Love

Love of others, love of mankind, love, and compassion for the world, and love of self are all ways of manifesting your brand of poise in your day-to-day life.

Women with poise do not necessarily have all the answers nor do they have their lives in perfect balance. However, they do know how to live with the uncertainties of life and recognize the importance of being clear on the direction of their work.

One who was a shining example, a masterpiece of grace and poise, one of the most recognized persons in history, is Mother Teresa. A champion of the poor and suffering in Calcutta and eventually all over the world, she certainly demonstrated that poise is not about the outer self; the good work of the inner core drives our deeds. When she eventually won the Nobel Peace Prize, she saw it not as a personal honor, but as recognition of the existence of the poor in the world and the importance of helping them.

I found this quote by Diane Ackerman years ago and it has become the theme and mission I live by: "I don't want to get to the end of my life and find that I lived just the length of it. I want to have lived the width of it as well." My wish is that your life will be blessed with deep richness, sharing love for others. I wish for you the wisdom, understanding, and authentic love that create true poise.

Transforming the Stories We Tell Ourselves As Women

by M. Bridget Cook-Burch
New York Times bestselling author

"What stories have I loved and believed in that have created possibilities—and limitations—for me?"

Storytellers love the magic of words, because they know that by weaving them in a certain way, the deepest part of our souls can be profoundly moved and changed forever. For centuries storytellers kept our history, and it is by telling stories that we as women have passed down the most vital tales about what it means to be a woman. Most often, those stories defined and determined what our roles and limitations should be, from the family to the community and into the workplace. However, certain women of courage throughout the ages learned to break free of those predetermined roles and to live lives of authenticity, empowerment, and transformation.

We can, too.

First, however, it is vital to determine exactly where our beliefs about women and about ourselves individually stem from. Parents, teachers, church leaders, mentors, and extended family all have played a role in weaving the stories we tell ourselves. As a student of politics and history, religion, philosophy, psychology, and economics, I have sought out the many reasons women believe the way they do about themselves, particularly their roles and their destiny within their communities. I once heard a quote by Harold Goddard that moved my blood: "The destiny of the world is determined less by the battles that are lost and won than by the stories it loves and believes in."

What sublime truth resides in that one small sentence! Loving and believing in certain stories can affect our behavior—consciously or unconsciously—on a daily basis. With such stories playing enormous starring roles in the chapters of our lives, there comes a time when it is wise to ask ourselves, "What stories have I loved and believed in that have created exciting possibilities for me? And what stories may have created psychological ceilings, walls, and limits for me?"

At the beginning of my writing career, I had the opportunity to write the tales of high-risk youth: the more successful stories of young women and young men seeking desperately to change their lives from circumstances that were often horrific. Many came from multigenerational gang-related families, where nearly every family member was a part of the gang. In those cases, the gang beliefs even superseded previous religious beliefs, where gang indoctrination had totally become their religion. The stories that developed around this violent lifestyle created a "box of beliefs" inside of which members were forced to live. It broke my heart to figure out what that meant for these vibrant, young beings full of new life and creativity. "Blood-in, blood-out" dogma meant they were forced to commit a violent, bloody crime to get in, and the only way out was to die for the cause or be killed if they wished to leave. It was quite shocking to me, and to others who had not grown up programmed in that particular way. I noticed a dangerous and unhealthy pattern in the way these gang members' stories so carefully justified where they were, why they were incarcerated, and who was to blame for their circumstances.

Their own stories quite literally bound and shackled them.

Still, I had the opportunity to witness the miraculous. When some of those youths were courageous enough to look honestly and openly at the stories of their lives . . . it was like an elixir of life. They could be open to new and wonderful possibilities, and I saw light fill their eyes. In fact, young lives started to transform before me the exact moment they realized they actually had choices.

"You mean I don't have to sleep with my gang leader just because he says so?" asked one young lady. Up until that moment, bound by her personal and communal stories, she did not even know she had real choices. At that moment, she became my teacher, for I learned a valuable truth: If a woman does not know she has a choice, she literally has no choice! However, the moment a woman's eyes are opened to see, the power can be put back into her own hands. I realized then that when any woman becomes empowered to be the author of her own story, she has the ability to rise, like a phoenix from the ashes of her previous life into a new world of possibility, self-love, and eventually, incredible outward contribution to the world around her.

I had the opportunity to write about the life of one such extraordinary young woman who was not a gang member but had come from equally harsh circumstances. Her name was Melissa G. Moore, and like many of us, she unconsciously held onto the stories about where she came from and what she was bound to do. Her stories were cemented in pain and anguish. Like many true tales I scribe, *Shattered Silence* was a story of great extremes. You see, Melissa was the daughter of a serial killer.

Can you imagine what stories you would tell yourself if you found out that your father was a serial killer? What labels would you give yourself knowing your own father had committed unspeakable acts upon women, holding absolutely no shame or remorse for those acts and even desiring credit for them? Can you imagine your fear in people finding out who you were related to? We have all heard it, "The apple doesn't fall far from the tree." People immediately treated her and her family members with great derision based only on association and not their own beliefs or behaviors. It validated her feelings of unworthiness. Therefore, as she went on into adulthood, Melissa told only a small handful of people, including her husband, where she had come from and who her father was. She told herself it was not safe to shine, that she had to play really "small" in life—to be a wallflower, almost unnoticeable. Even worse, she believed that because of who her father was, she was flawed. She was somehow to blame. She was not worthy of happiness. No matter how hard she tried on the outside, these stories wormed their way into everyday patterns of behavior. They got in the way of her living a happy and healthy life. She believed her stories and like so many of us, she played them out well.

From time to time, however, a divine spark within Melissa would not be denied. When she became the mother of a precious little girl and boy, her old stories would no longer hold up to scrutiny. As a compassionate mother, Melissa looked with great love upon her beautiful children. That divine spark deep within her awoke and blazed with a heat that would not be denied, and she burned with the knowledge that her beloved children were not flawed simply because of choices their grandfather had made. So, if that was true, how was it that Melissa, in her mind, could be so flawed?

Through hard, personal work, magical moments of introspection, and the fire within her that compelled her to take action, Melissa discovered that she herself had choices. One of those choices could be to live a life free of the guilt and shame that her father would not accept for himself, and that she had taken in his stead. She realized that her father's own self-limiting anger and victimhood had led him on a path of narcissism and destruction. Melissa's story was not all told; more powerful and profound chapters were to come. Melissa learned to become the captain of her own soul, the maker of her own choices—her own destiny—and by doing so became the "shero" of her own story!

Melissa did not know it at the time, but her struggle was a powerful example of courage and inspiration to me during a very dark time. As a newly single mom, I allowed my story to be unwritten, with many new chapters yet to live and to explore and to write. I began to shrug off the role of victim and chose instead to be a victor. Not over someone else . . . simply over my circumstances and the limiting beliefs that had led me to that particular, challenging chapter.

I discovered, however, that it would take conscious effort to disengage from old stories and old habits in all areas of my life. When I finally began dating after my divorce, I learned quickly to consciously engage in much healthier patterns of behavior. In dating it seemed easy, because I was hyper-vigilant not to create old patterns of abuse and codependency. However, when these patterns showed up in the workplace, I had a harder time breaking away, especially due to my desperate need to provide for my young children.

The story I believed in was that my job as a contractor was the only one that would provide a decent living so I could work from home and still provide food, emotional safety, and shelter for my children. However, repeatedly my client pushed boundaries and began sexually harassing me in conversations and e-mails. Finally, I spoke boldly to him, and he apologized. He actually behaved better for several weeks. I was relieved . . . until he tried to do online in the virtual world what I would not allow in person. Using an avatar, he visited the online site I was setting up for his business and made sexual advances toward my avatar. Although none of this interaction was "real," it felt all too real to me, and I felt violated and full of fear and shame every time he approached me. It got worse each day; he sought to override my objections, belittling my protests as naive, overblown, or even paranoid. I started to question my own discernment.

One day, however, when he came onscreen to direct me on an advertising initiative for his business, he again began his sexual innuendoes, and I was forced to hide his objectionable words and behavior on the computer from my own children! I felt so ashamed! I realized I had repeatedly allowed my boundaries to be crossed, a little at a time. Had I learned nothing at all?

While I had not been excited about my work for quite some time, I was horrified to now feel that I had to hide it. I did not want to have to live with shame every day. How could I work for a person who did not respect me enough to recognize my value as a professional and as a woman with real and solid boundaries. I wanted valuable work that was fulfilling and uplifting, and that I could take pride in showing my children.

Frustrated at myself and infuriated at my circumstances, I asked myself how I had been caught in this situation. I knew better! I was terrified by the prospect of firing my client. How could I support my children?

In spite of my fear, I tried to put my situation in perspective. I considered the lives of women I had studied throughout history. These women had sacrificed themselves for their children; compromised themselves in order to protect or care for their children; but most importantly, built a better world, the one that I was now living in, filled with freedoms and opportunities. The question seemed clear: Was I really stuck, or did I have many more choices that my eyes had simply not been open to see?

Stunned by my sudden awareness of the stories I had told myself up to that moment, I became filled with the powerful realization that I had hundreds, even thousands of possibilities. I went home, took a deep breath, and promptly fired my client! I did not know how I was going to make my next house payment. I did not even know how I would feed my children the next week, but with clear intention, I took back my power, and I honored the choices of the women who had come before me. I also chose to break the chains of my limitations. I stepped off the proverbial cliff and found that I had wings to fly.

Within days, an astounding number of business opportunities came my way. In awe of my actions, I discovered that I had transformed. Once unable to own my voice with a man, I partnered with a friend, a powerfully strong man, to develop and operate a successful, thriving trucking company. It required me to effectively hire, train, and manage many men and women on my staff. In directly facing my fears, I learned the true meaning of win-win, the most powerful form of transformation and healing in relationships. In what most consider a rough industry, I learned to live authentically, with a firm grasp on my boundaries, and to create something extraordinary in business and in a partnership.

Being open to new possibilities actually brought me an extraordinary opportunity. Not long after *Shattered Silence* was published, I was asked to write another story that I knew could forever leave a footprint on the hearts of women throughout the world. Rebecca Musser had been born and raised within an extreme cult in Utah. The story she had told herself as a young girl was that every self-sacrifice would be the refiner's fire to make her worthy of Heaven, which she and her people strived for above all other things.

In line with these beliefs, nineteen-year-old Rebecca was forced to marry her prophet—an eighty-five-year-old man with a greater-than-kinglike status among their polygamous people, the Fundamentalist Church of Jesus Christ of Latter-Day Saints, or FLDS. Rebecca became the nineteenth wife of a man who would eventually wed sixty-five women. As a woman in that society, she was given few choices, but when her husband died, she faced the hardest choice of them all: to continue to be repeatedly violated in the name of God, or to leave her entire family in order to claim her own life. This sheroic choice eventually led her to testify compassionately on behalf of faceless and voiceless young girls still living under horrific conditions in the community she had escaped from. Her life story, *The Witness Wore Red: The 19th Wife Who Brought Polygamous Cult Leaders to Justice*, is exceptionally inspiring.

Considering the powerful examples of Melissa and Rebecca, I take Goddard's quote and turn it into a question to women everywhere. What if your destiny is determined less by the battles lost and won than by the stories you love and believe in? What stories have you told yourself up until this moment? What labels have you lived by? What limitations have you placed upon yourself because of the stories of those who came before you—even those who loved you and simply did not know better?

That brings us to the most important question:

What new, empowering stories of love, honor, and celebration could you tell with awakened eyes and an authentic heart?

What powerful new places of possibility could you hold for yourself, congruent with your heart and your highest aspirations?

Like striking a match to kindling, having the courage to ask ourselves these loaded questions can ignite amazing inner conversations. Our most painful secrets and toughest challenges can be perfect catalysts for transformation, as those who have faced the most darkness have the ability to embrace the most light. That is why I invite all of us, as women of the world, to take the pen back. Are we yet written? No! More tales are to be woven, adventures to be had, and sheroes to be forged within the refiner's fire. For it is our hard-won dreams that breathe the most life into new possibilities for ourselves, and for all those who will follow. What gifts will you give your daughters, granddaughters, and great-granddaughters to ignite their flames of courage and truth?

Stories will continue throughout the coming ages of time. May yours be transformational. May they be sheroic!

How Women Can Hit the Bull's-Eye with Courage (Every Time)

by Sandra Ford Walston
The Courage Expert

"The bull's-eye that we women must learn to hit consistently is the true self"

When we think of courage in present-day society, we instantly see images of a superhero slaying bad guys or a soldier braving an onslaught of enemy fire. Yet the origin of courage is much closer to the actions that we take every day. Aristotle reminds us, "Courage is the first of human virtues because it makes all the other virtues possible." The reason courage is the first virtue is that it comes from the heart. The true meaning of the word *courage* comes from the French word *corage*, meaning "heart and spirit." Therefore, acting with courage is about acting from the heart, from the center of your innermost being. Another way of looking at this courage-centeredness is to think of what it takes to hit a bull's-eye.

We all know that hitting the bull's-eye means being on target, but have you ever wondered where the term comes from? Seventeenth-century English longbow yeomen in small hamlets often held archery practice immediately after church services, the only time during the week when many of the archers could gather. Wiktionary says the common target in those days was the white skull of a bull, and the greatest skill was demonstrated by hitting a "bull's eye." Hitting the target is one thing, but consistently putting arrows in the bull's-eye requires enormous practice.

The same holds true for anything else in life:

Achieving a high level of competence requires disciplined training to develop a certain set of "real" skills.

However, the challenge of courage-centeredness is to know that we are aiming at the right target. Unfortunately, far too many women who intuitively recognize the target distrust their own vision and aim in the wrong direction.

Ironically, the bull's-eye that we women must learn to hit consistently is the true self. Even when we do hit the target, women have to learn to recognize that everything outside the bull's-eye represents a different aspect of the false self (the ego or mind). The false self limits us. It fills us with self-doubt and fear of failure. By focusing on the bull's-eye of our true self, we access the empowering virtue of courage. We not only take aim at the true target of our life's work, we begin to hit the bull's-eye with ease. Naturally being more on target makes us happier and more self-fulfilled.

Are You Off Target?

Do you cherish your work? If you could choose to do a job that you would love to do, what would your heart's wish be? I have yet to meet a person who does not wish to be happy at work, but the most recent Gallup poll records that less than half of employees report overall job satisfaction. If you are disengaged at work, reflect on your aim and bring your own goal into view. Practice developing the skills that manifest courage at work and you will slice through your lack of self-contentment.

A perfect example of this is Sara who knows from experience how easy it is to get off target. In high school and college, she excelled in math and science. She entered college as an engineering major at the advice of guidance counselors and family members. She excelled scholastically and earned a doctorate in bioengineering. Despite never feeling any passion for her work, she was reluctant to change career paths, and in this state of unhappiness, she developed a severe eating disorder. She said, "My passion finally emerged while I was being treated for my eating disorder. It became clear that my mission was to help others overcome their eating disorders." Turning down a six-figure salary, Sara returned to college to earn her counseling degree. It took years for Sara to find the courage to act from her heart—the place where self-acceptance lives. Said another way, her courage was alive and well in her original self. Once she accessed it, she hit the bull's-eye in two ways: she became more self-fulfilled, and she made an important impact by helping others who needed her guidance and support.

Getting Back to the Center

Exploring and understanding the internal terrain of your courage takes time and dedication just like becoming an archer who consistently hits the bull's-eye. Each time you miss the target, you learn more about your personal courage and the power of the unconscious. Additionally, with each bull's-eye attempt you become more keenly conscious of the skills that went into making the shot. Your aim is more focused. Finally, you gain familiarity through experience. You have seen it all before, but now you understand it better. You are actually developing courage consciousness.

Begin to examine your personal courage by asking yourself a few simple questions:

- Would you stay in a job you hate or do not believe in?
- Are you inclined to secure your physical safety despite great inconvenience?
- Would you hide a mistake because you "need" your job?
- Are you prone to selling your soul (and you know it)?

Honestly answering these questions allows you to assess your courage and its correlation to the number of missed shots. By quieting your mind and allowing yourself to focus on the bull's-eye, you will realize that you know your true self better than you let on. The problem is that most people want concrete answers and a quick fix. They want to take a courage pill, rather than embrace the ongoing process called meditative self-reflection. This reflective zone supports you while you dwell on the answers to simple but probing questions like the ones mentioned. When you confess in your heart and spirit that you have sold your soul there is no magic pill or instant gratification, only emotional and spiritual suffering.

If your job does not honor the convictions of your heart, your courage is restricted. Awakening your personal courage begins with learning to stop and reflect so that you live from the inside—the bull's-eye of your true being.

Lin Carson's story is an example of "the bull's-eye of your true being." Lin is a scholastic baker in Denver. Although she had a doctorate in cereal science and chemistry, she knew the corporate road with Nestlé or Kraft would eventually not fulfill her unique ideas. A true example of the courageous spirit of the female visionary, Lin wanted to open her own bread café and develop recipes with shorter baking times so customers could purchase them all day long hot from the oven. As a result, she has reaped intrinsic rewards from her efforts and pursued long-term self-fulfillment.

Deceptively Simple

The simplest actions can have a tremendous impact. The skilled archer pauses his or her breathing before releasing the arrow. The pause provides a space for reflection. It is a powerful tool that allows you to have goals, yet stay present to shift gears as needed. This is very different from "going with the flow" or living in complacency (a courage killer).

With the emergence of "spiritual courage" at work, the mind/ego will want to undermine your courageous intent. The spiritual journey requires being in the present. It is a trust in faith that propels you to continue growing. You become a witness to your attachment to results and learn to self-correct. You surrender your ego to a higher level of courage consciousness, and you begin to exist in a place "where courage meets grace."

As all this happens, humility steps in to replace arrogance and righteousness. The sacred within awakens.

The concepts presented here are deceptively simple. After all, how could something so easy work? In his 2005 article "Simple Courage," my colleague René Da Costa writes that people at all levels of work shun simplicity for complication. He shared two reasons: "Simplicity takes talent and dedication, and it requires a great deal of courage. It takes courage to advocate simplicity. Simplicity has nowhere to hide and neither do those who advocate it." We become courageous by being courageous, and that means learning how to hit the bull's-eye more frequently. It is that simple!

All you have to do is decide whether this forgotten virtue called courage is worth a steady stream of bull's-eyes. How do you start to discover and identify your courage at work? Women with courage develop new business models when the door to an old model closes or the existing model no longer works. When asked if they have courage, they respond with an enthusiastic "yes."

Such was the case with Regina, an entrepreneur from Minneapolis. When asked, "How do you apply courage with your business?" she said, "I step forward and upward. I never quit. I take risks to continually reinvent myself, which sometimes leads to redesigning the organization." Then she paused, smiled, and said, "Just like Madonna." Setting challenging goals and taking calculated risks reveal entrepreneurs' hearts and spirits. Because of their desires to live their dreams and succeed, they foster and draw from an innate reservoir of courage that leads them down the path to entrepreneurial success.

What would motivate you to explore where this ancient virtue fits into your work life? If you are receptive, you will find that sometimes you are on target and other times you are not even aiming at the target.

The courageous leader asks for the tough project that no one wants and stays focused daily on the results.

Bull's-Eye Strategies

How can you increase your accuracy and help other people in your organization nurture this same skill? Here are three bull's-eye strategies:

Determine Why You Are Living Off Target

If you are not consistently hitting the bull's-eye, you are probably being thrown off-center by your mind/ego. Start to notice if you are focusing on negative external factors rather than listening to the affirmation of your heart. Eckhart Tolle admonishes us in *The Power of Now* to "Say 'yes' to life—and see how life suddenly starts to work for you rather than against you." Are you willing to say "yes" to courage, to become centered in your courage? If you are stirred by this challenge, then assess, recognize, and employ your underutilized strengths so you hit the mark more often. If you desire to remove aspects of mindless conformity from your work experience, then these fundamental courage-centering techniques are key. Ultimately courage-centering enables you to create a joyful life free from the habits that drain your energy and restrict your spirit.

To awaken your courage, you will need to let go of some unhealthy habits such as complaining or accepting mediocrity.

As you invite an overall healthier perspective about who you are, you diminish the missed shots in your professional life. This takes energy, but developmental courage is the source of energy that makes life fulfilling! At this integral level of courage consciousness it is valuable to remember this wise saying: "What is held in the mind tends to manifest."

Enhance Your Accuracy with Some Form of Meditation

Courage-centering begins with learning to stop and reflect so that you live from the inside, from the core of your true being. Finding a meditation practice can help to reveal your unconscious motivations and awaken your courage. Meditation techniques promote focus, centeredness, and spiritual awareness. They put you in touch with your heart and spirit.

Each of us is different, so what works for me may not work for you. Proven meditative techniques, such as prayer, yoga, therapy, transcendental meditation, chakra balancing, reflective reading, playing a musical instrument, writing, and so on, help to remind you of your spirit. Adopting a contemplative discipline begins the practice of targeting the bull's-eye, the self, in all aspects of life.

Start to Underscore Your Bull's-Eyes

These are your defined behavioral competencies. You know you have scored when you feel energized about your work rather than dispirited (e.g., your interaction with people becomes more productive and generous). Soon, you will look around and you will observe other courageous people—the person who confronted a bully on behalf of a peer, the person who volunteered for a challenging project, the person who lifted her voice above the crowd to speak the truth, or the person who did a job (any job) well from her heart-centered courage.

The real example of centeredness lies in the noble and courageous actions of the everyday person like you and me! While our culture does not celebrate the courage you display in your day-to-day life, recognize how your bull's-eyes make a difference in society. Your manifestation of courage-centeredness provides an example to the people around you, making courage contagious and, ultimately, transforming the workplace! Are you willing to make courage your daily legacy?

The Burden of Greatness

by Marcia Reynolds, PsyD
President of Covisioning, LLC

*"The speed of change depends on how much you live in
a state of curiosity instead of certainty."*

The day the doctors told my father he could no longer work was
the day he accepted his death sentence. If he had lived a long
life and was terminally ill, maybe I could understand his death
wish. He was only fifty-nine. He had gone deaf due to a growing
brain tumor. Yet the doctors said the tumor was operable. There
was even a possibility that he could hear again. However, they
insisted he stop working. No matter how I tried to convince him
that he still had a good life left to live, I failed. I wanted to shake
him and tell him to fight as he had always taught me to do. The
moment he sensed my anger, he rolled over and said he needed
to sleep. The routine was the same every night for two weeks
before my father's death.

In my anger for his leaving me, I somehow missed the lesson
in my father's passing. My father could not be the retiree. He
could not free himself from the identity of being the successful
businessman. When he could no longer hold on to that identity,
he quit living. All he knew about life was to work hard, be the best,

and help others achieve their dreams if he could. He equated fun with achievement. He packed his free time with tasks, including being the president of every nonprofit group he belonged to. When he had to give up his formula for prestige, he gave up his will to survive. I desperately tried to help him see what else he could accomplish if he redefined his goals. I did not see that it was his addiction to achievement that was killing him.

It took me years to see that his legacy helped me to be wildly successful and almost killed me, too. I worked the night after his funeral, thinking that was what he would have wanted me to do. He wanted me to thrive, to succeed, and to show the world how great I was. I proceeded to be successful partly for myself and partly in honor of his dreams for me. Then one night twenty years after his passing, I was sitting in the dark in my living room. I did not have enough energy to turn on a light. I was forty-five years old. I owned a beautiful home plus two cars in the garage. I had plaques and pictures demonstrating that I had achieved worldwide fame. In the dark, none of that was visible. There was something missing that kept me from enjoying my life. I was tired, unhappy, and had no idea who I was.

The night I sat in my living room in the dark, I thought I was alone in my situation. I did not know there were a growing number of women just like me—confident, passionate, and successful, yet disillusioned, exhausted, and confused. With the best of intentions, our parents raised us to excel and our society persuaded us to achieve. Being ordinary was not an option.

A 2006 study, reported by Ina Wagner and Ruth Wodak in *Discourse & Society*, identifies how women's work achievements are defining their identities. This condition is different from the past; women used to be much better than men at leaving their work persona at the office. Now, for most professional women, their work is their life. We have graduated from seeing work as something that will pay the bills to experiencing our careers as an integral part of our identity. On the positive side, our "professional skin" is tougher than that of our predecessors. On the negative side, work has become all-consuming.

The change in behavior of women at work after mid-1980 is due to four societal shifts for women: the focus on self-esteem, which has enhanced our confidence; the increase of competitive sports for women, which strengthened the body as well as the mind; the push to earn advanced degrees, where we now outnumber men; and the expectation of notable career success.

For the first time in history, girls are being brought up to believe they can, and should, be something special.

In particular, we high-achievers integrated this message to mean that we must do something amazing before we die. Yet "amazing" is not defined, and with each achievement, our aspirations are pushed to a higher target. We confuse our life purpose with what gives us applause.

I have come to call this phenomenon the "Burden of Greatness." Since the goal of superstardom is as hard to define as it is to achieve, our restlessness rarely subsides. We wander from job to job, goal to goal, and sometimes, relationship to relationship. Even if we are aware of this phenomenon, we struggle designing a plan for our wandering impulses.

I grew up having to find something to excel at in a "sea of excellers." I had to be one of these—the smartest, the best looking, the most athletic, the most popular, the most creative, or even the funniest. Moreover, any combination of bests was even better. I was told never to accept being second best even if second best was a great performance. Hungry for attention, I always found something to brag about. I never let on how hard it was to be the best when there were other very smart, very attractive, and very talented girls in my class.

When I reached adolescence, I rebelled against the idea that I had to be the best little girl in the world. This rebellion led me to a path of drug abuse. Since I could not keep up with what I thought my parents wanted for me, I looked to the most popular kids for recognition instead. The most popular kids did drugs. Since I was still driven to be the best, I could not be a mediocre drug user; I had to be the best drug user with the best drugs. Eventually I became hostile, self-destructive, and out-of control.

Then a miracle occurred. I learned one of my greatest life lessons—if you don't know who you are, you will never be content with what you can do—in one of the darkest places on earth, a jail cell. A year after high school graduation, I ended up spending six months in jail for possession of narcotics, an experience I swore would never happen to me. In truth, the sentence saved my life.

I learned that scary strangers, called inmates, could be unexpected angels. In particular, the leader of the toughest gang decided I should be her friend. Vickie was a smart and vocal woman. She was also a mother and a daughter. I wrote poems for her to send to her family. She also liked to play cards, and I proved to be a great challenger. In truth, I think Vickie and I learned a lot from each other during the many nights we talked and played cards until morning. I persuaded her to take the GED classes offered in the jail. She made me promise to write about her someday. One day, when I was feeling particularly sorry for myself, she jumped at me, pinned my body to the wall, and said, "You have no idea who you are, do you? You are smart. You are strong. But for some God-knows-why reason, you care about people." She pointed to my heart. "When you can see what you are hiding in here . . ." she then pointed beyond the bars, "you'll figure out how to be happy out there."

That was my first lesson in understanding that *who I am is different from what I can accomplish*. I did not know who I was inside my shell of achievement. Even though I did not fully understand her message at that moment, her words gave me the gumption to put my life back on track when I was released.

In order to get some control over my life, I had to explore the dark side of my inheritance of excellence from my father by asking myself some very difficult questions. Even today, when I find myself working too hard, I ask myself:

- Who am I beyond my skills and knowledge? What characteristics do I possess that help me to triumph over difficulties? How can I apply these traits to the challenges I am facing today?
- Who would I be if I were to stop everything and give voice to my heart? What am I keeping in exile that needs to be free? If I did not have to be great, what path would I take?
- Is there a way to enjoy my restless rumblings without sacrificing love and peace of mind?
- What is my highest potential? I might be good at what I am doing, but am I doing my best work with the skills, gifts, and talents I possess?
- How can I wander with purpose and intention, knowing what difference I want to make and the mark I want to make?

These questions, and others like them, have initiated powerful discussions with my coaching clients as well as for me.

Today I realize that my father was not trying to force me to be successful. He was doing his best to make sure I would lead a happy life where I could experience my full potential. It took me many years to reprogram my brain to consciously choose how I commit my time and energy. Today, I can be successful, busy, and at peace.

Four Lessons from a Tire Iron

by Lisa Mininni
Bestselling author of *Me, Myself, and Why?*
The Secrets to Navigating Change, president
of Excellerate Associates, and host of
BlogTalkRadio's *Navigating Change*

"When you work in alignment with
who you are, it's not work."

As I glanced outside my kitchen window in the height of the economic storm, I thought, "Another cold December day." The whipping winds mirrored my work as an executive where I was navigating mergers, divestitures, and closures of facilities. The news finally hit like a crash of thunder. The division that I helped grow was being dismantled. This was when my entrepreneurial journey began.

As a high performer known for delivering outcomes, I mistakenly thought that it would only be a short time before I landed another corporate position. I had the experience, education, and was in the prime of my career. I had been promoted multiple times, and, surely, it would be a snap to find the same kind of job. While I had been busy working eighty hours a week, many things had shifted in the marketplace. Leads dried up fast. When I tried to get another traditional corporate job, I experienced many varied and unusual roadblocks. I was beginning to reconsider what to do for a living.

I struggled to assemble a daily routine and felt like I was swimming upstream in mud. On yet another cloudy December day, I summoned up the energy to meet a colleague to network. While driving down the freeway, I had a million thoughts on my mind. I considered different career options, and questioned, "Is writing a book and starting my own business the right decision?"

Suddenly, my thoughts scattered as something popped up from the freeway and headed straight for me. I instinctively put my arms in front of my face and heard a big whooshing sound and dinging in my front seat. I opened my eyes to find my windshield shattered by a softball-size hole and a four-foot, five-pound, semi-truck's tire iron in the front seat of my car. I navigated to the side of the road and steered to the nearest parking lot. Covered in pieces of glass, I stepped out of the car physically unhurt but then realized the real extent of the damage. There was a six-inch gash in the steel hood of the car. While examining the trajectory of the tire iron, I realized how fortunate I was. You see, thankfully the tire iron hit the hood first and changed the course of the tire iron—and mine. Yet, I was thinking, job loss, continuous rejection, and now this! Not a good time.

Three police officers soon arrived and said, "Lady, you're on this earth for a reason." Just moments earlier I questioned if starting a business and writing a book was the right decision; the tire iron got my attention so that I could receive this important message delivered by three police officers. This brings me to my first lesson.

Lesson #1: It Is for Your Greater Good

Navigating life's transitions was not new to me, but this life event seemed overwhelming. I realized years later that things work out in their perfect order. They do not seem perfect when we are experiencing them, but they prepare us for the next stage. Looking back, almost all of the positions I applied for eventually were either eliminated or the companies closed. I would have been going through the exact same career transition again if I had been offered any of those positions. I could not see it at the time, but being rejected for those jobs created the shift to consider entrepreneurship.

Therefore, what should you do when you are experiencing something unpleasant? Be grounded in knowing it is happening for your greater good. You're not going to be able to explain it, justify it, or even like it; just know there is something greater planned, something you cannot see right now. This mindset will get you through the present and give you a sense of calmness about your current circumstances. Likely, you will understand your experience years later. The roadblocks I experienced also paved the way to my second lesson.

Lesson #2: Release

Because of these roadblocks, I entertained the thought of switching from employee to entrepreneur. I embraced new discoveries about myself and aligned it with the work I did. In fact, I realized I naturally put together infrastructures and processes, something that aided my early corporate career. At the time, since I did not see any books that gave practical advice about navigating change, I began writing my own book, which integrated the process of navigating change with practical exercises that helped me create a foundation for life-long transformation.

I also started my own professional strategy practice—initially resisting business ownership—yet, at the same time, being motivated by it. Over time, I found that I loved the independence of entrepreneurship and the variety it provided. As an entrepreneur, this is one of the most important lessons to learn.

There will be times you need to release relationships, clients, and even belief systems about how to market. Releasing outdated belief systems is core to becoming a profitable entrepreneur.

While I was letting go of what was, it brought me to my third lesson.

Lesson #3: Walk in Faith

Have you noticed that when you are making a really big leap, your mind tends to think about what you have to give up rather than what you could gain? For example, when you want to shed some extra pounds, you think about what foods or habits you must give up, not how healthy you will be when you've done so. When you invest in your business, you look at the cost involved and not the new opportunities it will open up for you.

Early on in entrepreneurship, I hesitated to invest in my business, because I did not see how I was going to pay for it. I was thinking about right now and not walking with the confidence that the money will be there.

When I changed my mindset and walked with confidence that my resources will be there (and did not allow myself to get caught up in the small details of how something would happen), everything fell into place at the right time. Life became easier and more abundant.

Walking in faith is one of the most important shifts you can make when transforming yourself from employee to entrepreneur. What I learned is when you walk with fear rather than faith, it becomes a self-limiting mindset that stops you from becoming the best you. It delays your results and getting your gifts to those who need them most.

When you shift to the faith mindset, pieces fall into place even though you have not worked out the "how" yet. Years ago, I decided to take my business to the next level. I realized that I needed to free up my schedule and shift some of the nonrevenue and nonclient work to a trustworthy and reliable worker. I was not sure who that would be. One day out of the clear blue, the name of a friend popped into my head. In fact, I had worked with her many years ago and knew she had a strong work ethic. I am not sure why I did not think of her at first. It just hit me all of a sudden.

I thought that this friend might be interested in working from home since she had small children. When I asked if she might be interested, she started to laugh. Confused, I asked her what she was laughing about. She began to share with me that her church had been arranging a mission trip. She informed me that she felt a strong urge to go on this trip, but that it required a significant investment to pay for the travel expenses. She began to think about the family vacation they may not be able to take over the summer if she went, the effect her absence would have on her husband and children, and all of the little things she would have to give up if she went on this trip. She never stopped to think about what she would gain by going on the mission trip, just what she would be giving up.

She struggled to reach a decision because she was so focused on how she was going to make it happen. At last, she decided it was the right thing to do. She signed up and wrote out a check, even though she had no additional income to pay for it. She just took a leap of faith.

Within days of writing the check, she received a call from several neighbors asking her to clean their homes as well as my call to help with my business. The how showed up. It was because she started the flow by releasing and walking in faith.

My friend went on her mission trip to Guatemala helping build homes for homeless women and children. The Guatemalan community was helped by her involvement and my friend helped me. In addition, I was able to help a lot more clients so they could continue doing their work.

The next time you are thinking about taking a really big leap, but you are getting caught up in the how, walk in faith.

People are praying for a solution that you provide with your business. It is up to you to make sure they find you.

Consider all of those who would not be helped by you retreating back into your comfort zone. If the Wright brothers had kept their inventions to themselves, millions of people would not have traveled to their freedom, discovered work that provided for their families, or launched related businesses that, in turn, improved the world.

Think about the bigger picture. It may not be entirely about you but about a series of events that include you as you pursue a much bigger mission.

Stepping in faith involves conviction that everything is evolving and aligning every day. Leaping into faith is a lot like baking a cake. You put the ingredients together and heat it at the right temperature. You cannot always see the transformation happening, but with a little patience, you get a pretty sweet dessert.

As you start to take these leaps of faith, you will start looking ahead and *envisioning things you had not thought of before.*

Lesson #4: Imagine the Possibilities

When you are taking a leap of faith, imagine the possibilities and outcomes. Allow yourself to pass through the fear and walk into the place beyond the fear. Picture this "after" place when you are in the process of making the change. Imagine what you will feel like, accomplish, and gain when you do take a step forward.

During the process of transforming from employee to entrepreneur, I learned about my innate strengths of creating simplicity out of confusion and that I create systems and structure from chaos. Like an architect that creates the blueprint to guide construction, I discovered that I help others design a foundation they can build on.

I started to imagine becoming a bestselling, self-published author. I did not even know that was possible, but people kept arriving into my life that got me closer to becoming a bestseller. It started with the vision. Then, page by page, I penned away through my book. It took five years, but I finally released my book internationally, and it became a category bestseller right next to Jack Canfield's *Chicken Soup for the Soul* and John Gray's *Men Are from Mars, Women Are from Venus*. It continues to sell today.

I kept on imagining new possibilities. I learned different applications for skills I already had. I used my interviewing skills with other bestselling authors on my Internet radio show, which expanded to thousands of listeners around the world and reached entrepreneurs in more than eleven countries. My process improvement background served me in developing ways small business owners could bring in prequalified prospects and turn them into invested clients 98 percent of the time.

I realize that every experience, every natural talent, every learned skill prepared me for this very moment in life. I discovered that "when you work in alignment with who you are, it's not work."

While in the cloud of my change, I did not know where this alternative path was leading, but I kept moving forward in faith. When I had nothing left emotionally, faith gave me the courage, calmness, and confidence to reveal my authentic self. I realize now these were all defining moments. The thing I needed to change was how I saw them, and so it is with you.

The Power of Perspective and Perception

by Kristin Andress
Strategist and consultant

"When you focus on mastering your mind, and thus your perceptions and perspective, you discover different paths in the landscape of your possibilities."

How we view our lives and the world we live in makes the difference in how we relate to ourselves and to others. I was once in Bangladesh with my business partner and we met with two monks at different times. In each case, their guidance was the same, "Master your mind. Shift your gaze." Our experience is shaped by how we choose to perceive the world.

Framing and reframing your experiences in life can prevent you from spiraling into a vortex of anxiety or despair. The ability to catch yourself when you get that sinking feeling lies in being aware that it is happening, and choosing to pause and select a new perspective. This is much more than seeing the glass half full or making lemons into lemonade. It is a matter of deciding how you will integrate your way of "being" into your life and lifestyle. The power to reflect on your perspective and reframe it gives you an opening to see the world, other people, and yourself in different ways. Typically, it is a much more peaceful and satisfying way. Following are a few examples.

Experience Joy for What You Have

We crossed a lagoon in a canoe and landed on a twenty-eight-mile beach in remote Cox's Bazar, Bangladesh. Within minutes of our arrival, barely clothed, native children surrounded us. They approached us with no hesitancy, complete curiosity, and big, beautiful smiles. One little girl was enthralled with a book I was carrying. I imagine it was the first one she had seen. Another girl packed her little brother on her hip. I don't believe he was old enough to walk, yet she did not appear to mind his weight. She seemed to embrace that her brother was simply her responsibility each day.

Another little boy was playing with the red ocean crabs that cover the beach, holding two of them in the air as if they were about to fight. As the children gathered around, my business partner taught them to yodel, and we taught them the sign language gesture for love. They laughed and laughed with us. We were struck by their lack of schooling and even clothing, yet they demonstrated joy in simply being with each other and us. Certainly, we were reminded to be grateful for our abundance and mindful that we could be unhappy with much, or happy with little.

There were no adults in sight; they were off fishing to have something to sell, and for their children's evening dinner. These kids did not know they had little. They made much out of that little. They were full of joy. There is a saying, "You don't know what you don't know." I am proud of these children. Their perception is, "This is my world." Their perspective is, "And, it's just fine with me." In our modern world, we become aware of what we do not have and often forget to appreciate all that we do have.

Give First

In high school, I was a member of the student council. Each year around Christmas we delivered food and toys to the poor, and I will never forget one particular year. We drove down a snow-covered gravel road to one of the "needy" homes. The cold and gray day began to color our mood. The good news was we got to cut afternoon classes to make these deliveries. We gave little thought for the people whose lives we would soon touch. We only planned to get done fast and goof off. We bounced over a hill in a rusted old car with a hatchback full of toys and food. A rundown two-story house scarred the top of the next crest. A dilapidated barn sagged nearby; thin curtains hung sparsely in the windows. A leafless oak stretched barren limbs over a rutted drive, empty of cars. Caving cement steps warned trespassers to step carefully onto the rickety porch.

We each carried a box. An older man opened the latchless ripped screen door, his thin smile and downcast eyes conveying a sense of shame. After an uncomfortable moment, he stepped away and allowed us to enter with our gifts. A child appeared, a sandy blond boy, and he bounced when he yelled, "They're here! They're here!" No one, unless it was Santa himself, could have told him we would visit.

His little sister appeared not far behind him, thumb in her mouth, her dark eyes wide with curiosity, and blonde ringlets pressed to rosy cheeks. The pajama-clad boy ran to us before we could speak. The home danced with his excitement as he chose his first toy from the box nearest the door. As quickly, he knelt to one knee and extended his discovery gently with both hands. "Look! Look! This is what you asked for. You got it! You got it!" He presented the prize to his sister, a hoped-for baton she could twirl and throw.

A smile replaced the thumb in the girl's mouth. The smile, so angelic, compared only to that of the little shepherd beside her, her brother. The embrace between them thawed our hurried hearts. The boy did not rush to see what we had brought for him. Instead, he enjoyed most his sister's pleasure in her baton.

We left that day, our footsteps slower than when we arrived. He gave us the greater gift, perhaps, by showing us how to give first, and willingly.

Choices: How Do You See the Happenings of Your Life?

Many years ago, my brother died of a self-inflicted gunshot wound. Unlike some illnesses, during which we have time to prepare for a loss, this was a shock. We grieved, of course. We argued and felt guilty about how we might have prevented his death. After a period of grieving his death, we reframed the situation to ask ourselves, how would he prefer we live? What could we do to honor his memory? Then we celebrated his life by doing something for ourselves and for others. We created a children's fund for delivering toys and coats at Christmas. It was a way for us to release our pain and grief and instead build more positive experiences around his memory.

I have learned that the way we see things makes the difference. We can turn the trials and tribulations into triumphs. Changing your viewpoint may not remove the sadness of missing someone or something, but giving your thoughts over to a new perspective, taking action on it and giving of yourself can create a positive legacy even from irretrievable loss.

Reframe Your Assumptions/Expectations

How many times have you dreaded going somewhere only to discover that once you arrived, you enjoyed it? We often make assumptions about what an experience will or will not be, but the truth is we will not know unless we try. I am a nervous flyer, and sometimes trekking through airports, finding seats and overhead spaces on planes, locating the taxi line, and getting to hotels is just a stressful hassle. Sometimes I have allowed my apprehension about that process to stop me, no matter how great the destination might be. I have either decided not to go or I have been anxiety-ridden days in advance, rather than just enjoying the nontravel days. I have promised myself that next time it happens I will change my perspective and reframe it. Instead of obsessing about my fears, I will shift my attention outside myself to discover:

- Who can I meet en route?
- How do I want to make others feel?
- Who might need my help with a bag, a stroller, or a door?
- How can I make it fun for others and for myself?

I am going to perceive the process and the outcome as an experience I can personally influence and create. In addition, I am going to feel so much better because I did. It is not our responsibility to see others or do for them, but each encounter creates an opportunity for peaceful, satisfying, and fulfilling relationships.

You may not believe that a simple shift in your choice of perspective and perceptions can cause a massive shift in the path you are on and the purpose you feel while on it. However, I hope you will give it a try and see what happens.

Give This Some Thought

"You are looking the wrong way!" That can mean so many things. What are you missing when you do not see or when you are not aware? I wonder what would happen if I shifted my perception of what my life is or can be. I wonder what could happen if I chose to be different in my day-to-day routine. This has nothing, necessarily, to do with doing something different. This is about you. It is not even about success, unless it is a reflection of how you define what success looks like for you. This is about who you are as a person, how you choose to inhabit your life, and how you decide to relate to your world and the people in this bigger Being of Humanity. There is a Sanskrit word, *Vismaya*, which means, "astonished or overwhelmed with a sense of wonder."

Imagine being astonished by what is within and around you. What would that perception, if experienced with your whole being, create for you? If all of us felt that way, how would that change the world?

Sometimes a change of perspective and realizing the power of your perceptions starts simply with conscious thought, asking yourself a few questions, and engaging in some healthy internal dialogue. This contemplation can help us realize we need not all be exactly the same. In fact, our differences can escalate our innovations, our accomplishments, and our contribution to solving bigger issues than we can by ourselves.

I invite you to think about it.

What Do You Receive?

When you focus on mastering your mind, and thus your perceptions and perspective, you discover different paths in the landscape of your possibilities. You naturally think differently. You behave with a positive energy that attracts good things in personal and business relationships. Rather than stumbling down a rabbit hole of cynicism, fear, anxiety, judgment, or blame, which is often the result of habitual behavior and routinized thinking, you receive:

- Acceptance of self and others
- Abundance in place of scarcity
- Expanding possibilities
- The facts
- Understanding that your thoughts and perceptions affect the quality of your life

Aren't many of us (who are like-minded and like-spirited) really on a quest for peacefulness? We desire less stress, less anxiety, more connection, and fewer worries, all of which result in a sense of peace within. How do we cultivate peacefulness? Do we remember how it feels?

How can you invite it in? Know that it exists. All you need to do is open to receive it.

Live in Big Love

One of my favorite books is Marianne Williamson's *A Return to Love*. I appreciate so many passages, but one I think of most is about Avalon. Avalon is an enchanted realm like the ones we imagined as children. It exists beyond the vision of our physical eyes and cannot be seen without faith first. Once we believe it exists, the mists our mind has created part and allow us to see Avalon. Belief or faith is the first step toward willingness to perceive in a new or different way. Now, I do not claim that the power of your perspective and perceptions will create a Utopia like Avalon, although it will help you sift through the stuff of life to what is real and place you in a realm of understanding of what really matters. Shifting your perspective will open your heart to yourself and to others and bring you the gem of love. Big love is love in its highest sense, the sense that comes with your opportunity to choose who you are—every day—and how you will "be" in this lifetime.

The New Beauty Paradox

by Vivian Diller, PhD, with Michele Willens
Authors of *Face It: What Women Really Feel
As Their Looks Change*

*"Attractiveness is about what is outside and inside,
and what counts most is connecting the two."*

Is this what we fought for? Beauty is antithetical to our democratic ideals. It is distributed unfairly and unequally and this does not sit well with other values held by most evolved women. Consequently, many of us deal with the subject of beauty by dismissing it as antifeminist, unintellectual, and culturally induced. Others hold contempt for those who are blessed with great genes. Some just cope by using cognitive dissonance, a mental trick that allows us to feel more comfortable with a reality we cannot control: concluding, for example, that most beautiful women are stupid. Sure, we have occasionally heard of the brainy blonde but not nearly as often as her dumb counterpart.

In spite of these cognitive acrobatics and rationalizations, many of us continue to struggle in reconciling who we are with how we look. Why does our appearance matter to us even if our politics, beliefs, and intellect tell us it should not? To understand this dilemma, we have to recognize the biological and cultural roles beauty plays in our lives.

What has always been—and remains—true is that beauty, in its purest sense, is a universal staple of human experience. It plays a powerful and fundamental role in our personal and professional lives. It is a basic human pleasure that will never go away.

Scientific studies have been conducted to demonstrate that humans are hardwired to react to beauty. Recent research supports the belief that attractive physical features serve evolution, propelling the survival of our species. Psycho-sociologists examining the psychology of beauty infer that people who are commonly considered attractive seem to survive better than those who are not. Geoffrey Cowley reported in his *Newsweek* article "The Biology of Beauty" that this research has led psychosociologists to theorize that good-looking people may have stronger immune systems, more robust genes, and higher mate value. Other studies tell us that what is considered attractive is similar across varied and unrelated cultures. For example, Dario Maestripieri found that men generally are more attracted to women with large eyes and small noses set in round faces—features often associated with infants. Itzhak Aharon and others wrote in the journal *Neuron* that MRI and PET scans provide further evidence about the importance of beauty: Female brain activity has been shown to increase when women are told they are being admired by men. Male brains register more activity when viewing women they consider attractive.

Developmental research by C.A. Samuels and others reveals that newborns not only quickly recognize facial features but also demonstrate preference for faces independently rated as attractive. This natural bias for beauty evolves into deep-seated stereotypes that result in a psychological phenomenon called the "halo effect," which determines that the quality of one trait is applied automatically to all parts of the object being observed.

For example, Arthur Miller wrote that someone who is regarded as beautiful is also assumed to be responsible, intelligent, adaptable, and so on. Kate Fox notes that this translates into a tendency for attractive people to be hired faster, get better jobs, earn more money, and even get acquitted more often. In essence, those who are physically blessed are not simply accorded more leeway in life, they are universally and positively recognized and rewarded.

It is not surprising then that the desire to be attractive and perceived as such remains important to women of all ages across the world and spans all ages. Sociologist Naomi Wolf writes, "Beauty is a currency system like the gold standard." Most women agree, reporting that good looks continue to be associated with respect, legitimacy, and power in their relationships with others. Actress and model Isabella Rossellini says, "In monetary terms, beauty pays more than anything."

What do these facts and inequities about physical beauty mean to a generation of women whose childlike faces are fast becoming distant memories? It could lead you to conclude that we are right back where we started, with science confirming the sentiment supported by so many popular books—that it is what's outside that counts and that we should, in fact, seek ways not to look old. Or, accept our biology and resign ourselves to an inevitable fate, as Lucille Ball jokingly suggested: "The secret of staying younger is to live honestly, eat slowly, and lie about your age." Easy to say, but it is not so simple.

To truly understand beauty is to view it as a combination of objectivity and perception, as a science and an art. Some studies demonstrate that how we appear to others is about more than what meets the eye. For example, one study by Nisbett and Wilson found that college students rated a professor as physically attractive when he behaved with kindness; whereas, when the same instructor seemed cold and distant, they did not. In another study Hoover and Arkkelin examined attributes used to select a mate and found that physical features were viewed as having less value than qualities like seriousness, sincerity, and independence. For both men and women, finding a partner with whom they could develop a committed relationship was considered more important than finding one with good looks. An international survey of women by Nancy Etcoff and others in 2004 suggests that, in most countries, only a small percentage are comfortable calling themselves beautiful, but many call themselves attractive if they are engaged in enjoyable activities and have close relationships.

In my own research, when women were asked the question, "At what time in your life did you view yourself as most attractive?" many answers were remarkably unrelated to a specific age. A majority said it was in their twenties or thirties, but many responded that they felt most attractive later in life, when they felt more confident or when they were happiest.

Findings from studies on beauty confirm what most of us know, that experience of attractiveness is about what is outside and inside, and what counts most is connecting the two. It is this very connection that millions of us are finding so hard to make.

One might take comfort in the fact that our physical ideal of beauty holds greater contradictions today than ever before. Women sporting holes in jeans, rings through noses, and multicolored braids are seen on the covers of current fashion magazines. In contrast to traditional images that have featured facial and body symmetry, there is now great variation in what constitutes good looks: the ultrathin, ultratall, the curvy, the bony, the straight haired, the curly, the spiky, and on it goes.

Moreover, public fascination with physical appearances currently flips as quickly as our remote controls—from Miss America to *The Biggest Loser*. *America's Next Top Model* explicitly tried to broaden the criteria for their contestants. By inviting women under five feet seven inches to audition, they hoped to interest a greater variety of competitors seeking a spot on their show. The result? Bedlam, as hundreds of everyday, good-looking women flooded the audition, fighting for the chance to be acknowledged as the most beautiful.

You would think that all this opportunity and variety might represent a form of emancipation!

Yet among all these new variations there remains one constant that does not fluctuate in our culture or in our minds: *Youth.* Young, clear, unblemished skin and strong, smooth bodies remain the ideal image to which women feel driven. It is a visual ideal no longer confined to the province of young brides, celebrities, or fashion models. Women of all ages and walks of life are drawn toward this narrow definition of beauty at any cost and by whatever means.

Instead of equality, we have this daunting equation: If beauty equals youth, and aging equals the loss of youth, how can an older woman feel good about herself? Small wonder we are confused about the messages we are receiving and the emotions we did not think we would be confronting.

Sure, millions turning forty exhaled when feminist leader Gloria Steinem responded to being told that she didn't look her age with, "This is what forty looks like. We have been lying for so long, who would know?" Yet ask most women and you will find that these milestones matter a great deal. With great fanfare, the toy industry celebrated Barbie's fiftieth birthday in 2009. Not surprisingly, this anatomically admired doll remains remarkably unchanged from the one we played with when we were little girls. Is this what we fought for? On paper, we may claim it is unfair: Why are we allowed to grow up but not grow older? Publicly we defy the inequity and deny the power of our youth-defined culture, while in reality it confronts us with enormous challenges. The antiaging movement is a billion dollar industry and continues to be the road sought by most women today.

A New Movement: Somewhere Between Feminism and Narcissism

For years, the women's movement focused on freeing more than half our population from the traps of sexism and discrimination. As a result, women today continue to crash higher glass ceilings and break new barriers at every turn. We are a proud generation, witnessed by the thunderous applause Hillary Clinton received as she acknowledged the "18 million cracks" her votes represented in the 2008 primary. Nevertheless, do we really think she ever stopped caring how she looked while doing all that crashing and breaking? Do any of us? No doubt even accomplished women feel stressed keeping pace with confident, resourceful younger women coming up from behind.

The sooner we realize that our changing looks play a real yet complex role in how we feel about ourselves, the better we will be able to manage. It is time we use our knowledge, experience, and fortitude to change the way we deal with our changing appearance.

As Carla Bruni, former first lady of France said, "With aging, if there is no philosophy, there is no serenity, there's no wisdom, there's nothing but falling apart. Wrinkles without wisdom is boredom." The good news is that we have created a society where, as successful women, we are mostly admired for our years of hard work.

Look at the well-earned kudos handed to Nancy Pelosi, Arianna Huffington, Meryl Streep, and Oprah Winfrey to name a few. These are not simply "beauty queens," but queens on a much broader scale. The bad news is that women are often marginalized if their experience shows on their faces. Colleagues whisper, "She needs some work." In the movie business, they say, "We need a young Glenn Close."

How much have female stereotypes really changed if, for instance, during Hillary Clinton's run for president, Rush Limbaugh can rhetorically ask his large listening audience, "Will Americans want to watch a woman get older before their eyes on a daily basis?" Have we really been liberated if more attention is paid to what women wear than what they say? Do people recall Sarah Palin's wardrobe or the content of her speeches—if we remember her at all? We only have to look at the 2014 list of the World's 100 Most Powerful Women, compiled by *Forbes*, to be reminded of the struggles we still face. To our credit, we see multiracial, black and white, but only nine are noticeably gray, four fewer than in 2012.

I propose a new movement that meshes feminism—and all freedoms we have gained as a result—with a bit of necessary narcissism. This fresh perspective does not call for being wedded to either of these philosophies, but it will require finding a healthy balance between them. It entails a change in attitude, perspective, and focus. It means caring for ourselves by allowing looks to matter but not so much that we forget to take care of our long-term, lifetime needs. In the end, our movement will lead to a new kind of freedom that takes into account both our internal and external selves, naturally blending the two.

As a generation, Baby Boomer women worked hard to change the culture in which we live. Now it's time to find a more dignified, thoughtful approach to our changing looks—to detoxify the cultural messages custom fitted to women's anxieties and talk out loud about the subject, openly and honestly.

We need not confine this dilemma to the comforting couches of psychotherapists, although we welcome that as one option, nor should we dump it in the deft hands of plastic surgeons. The challenge is not about how not to look our age, nor is it about seeking miracles to help us flee the facts. Make no mistake, we are not antisurgery, antipotions or peels, or anything else that allows us to feel better about ourselves. However, we are opposed to reacting thoughtlessly to external pressures about how we should look. We want women, who have broken through in so many arenas, to make decisions in this area with a similarly clear head and realistic expectations. Getting older was never a walk in the park, but it is particularly frightening to a generation of women who planned to stay "forever young." Once an appealing notion, these words have become a mandatory mantra. The challenge: can we keep youthful optimism in our hearts and minds while letting our faces follow their natural course?

We are strong, smart, and vital women who have been given the gift of time. Let us not waste another moment trying to stop the inevitable. Our clocks tick on no matter what we do—or do not do—to our faces and bodies. Instead, let us size up where we are physically and emotionally. Let us recognize the cultural confusion that makes it hard to move forward. Let us go beneath the surface so we can look thoughtfully at our options for dealing more effectively with aging.

Embrace this new movement and you will be able take advantage of the process described in my book, *Face It: What*

Women Really Feel As Their Looks Change. It describes the six psychological internal changes that bring greater acceptance of the inevitable external ones. You learn how to let go of a static self-image and replace it with a more flexible one that can change with age. One of the first steps is recognizing how hypercritical we are of ourselves, especially about our appearance. We would never be as judgmental about our friends, peers, or children as we are about the reflection we see in the mirror. Unless we become cognizant of this negative internal dialogue, it is hard to know how much we undermine our own self-confidence. Try looking in the mirror and talking to yourself the way you might a good friend and you'd be surprised how much better—and more attractive—you feel.

True empowerment comes from understanding that attractiveness plays a role in every woman's self-esteem, but must be balanced with the many other ways we can define ourselves as post-feminist women. Remember, our forebears were pioneers for women's rights, driven by a mission that took precedence over caring about our appearance. In today's world, we are free to seek high-powered careers and follow our passions without giving up our feminine identity. Ultimately, our goal is to enjoy our health and beauty from the inside and out so we can look and feel the best we can for the rest of our lives.

Ignite Your Life and Connect for a Better World

by Nancy D. O'Reilly, PsyD
Clinical psychologist, philanthropist,
and founder of WomenSpeak.com

*"Women often say, 'I don't have time!' but we need
to love and respect ourselves enough to take care of our
God-given bodies."*

Do you have all the power you need to create the satisfying
and rewarding life you want? If not, why not? Sometimes an
overwhelming external barrier keeps us from moving forward. If
that is your situation, you have my sympathy and my admiration
for your ability to cope. More often, we obstruct ourselves in
a myriad of ways. We rob ourselves of connections that could
sustain us and relationships that could bring us joy.

We may make choices that interfere with our ability to make
our dreams come true. We may allow life's circumstances (e.g.,
responsibility for our children and aging parents, the need for a
steady income or benefits) to put our dreams and aspirations on
hold, not to mention having a good time and enjoying ourselves.
Do you resonate with any of this? If so, are you willing to reassess

your priorities and take a good hard look at what you imagine you can become in this life?

None of us want to look back and regret the choices we made. Yet women tend to make choices to benefit everyone else in their lives before they commit to taking care of themselves and pursuing a passion and purpose of their own. It is not rocket science, but it takes determination and persistence to master the techniques of external power and internal power presented in the first two sections of this book. These techniques are the engines propelling your purpose. However, those powerful engines will only advance you to your goal if your guidance system is programmed correctly. If not, you may fly off course and even crash.

To live the most vibrant life possible, women must be able to pursue something they care deeply about. Each of us needs to learn what that is, chart her course, and keep her guidance system in good repair. The most effective tools I have found for doing this may seem elementary, but in my experience, they are essential. We must cultivate good habits for a healthy body, mind, and spirit. Daily attention to our own physical, mental, and emotional well-being forms the foundation for an accurate life map and supportive guidance system. If we shortchange ourselves in any of these areas for long, we become blocked, frustrated, or dissatisfied. Wouldn't you rather feel open, delighted, and fulfilled?

Wake Up

My own mission is to help other women connect with their passion in every way they can and to connect with each other to make the world a better place. In pursuing my mission, I met the Dalai Lama a few years ago. He impressed me when he said the future of the world rests in the hands of Western women. What a responsibility! He also said that before Western women could fulfill this destiny—to become the force that changes the world—we must wake up. We cannot change anything for the better or act responsibly if we do not open our eyes, minds, and hearts to the world we live in now.

Move It or Lose It

The number one, most important way to wake up to our world—bar none—is to get moving. We are spiritual beings in a temporal body, and our bodies are meant to move. Exercise helps keep us happy and healthy. If you feel tired, stiff, or in pain, you are unlikely to take on that next ambitious challenge. The less you do, the less you can do. To avoid that unfortunate fate, please, try various physical activities and find some you enjoy. Just move more today than you did yesterday. Seriously, that is all there is to it.

Exercise makes us feel happy and strong partly because it forces us to breathe deeply. Each in-breath, or "inspiration," brings fresh oxygen into your body and brain and you feel great. Working out when you feel tense is guaranteed to relieve stress and tension in your muscles and your mind. When you exercise, your body produces "happy hormones": norepinephrine makes you feel energetic, endorphins cheer you up, and serotonin helps you relax.

Regular exercise makes us healthier as well as happier. Every disease prevention program—whether focused on preventing cancer, heart disease, dementia, or autoimmune disorder—says we need regular exercise. It is even more important to our animal body than what we eat, although of course that matters too. We need to attend to both in order to achieve and maintain a healthy weight. It is not about being skinny; it is about being healthy.

Developing fitness habits for your lifetime is truly one of the best things you can do for yourself, your family, and for your cause. Women often say, "I don't have time!" but we need to love and respect ourselves enough to take care of our God-given bodies. Make a plan with another woman to exercise together and you will have the added benefit of sharing your experiences and support.

Stay Present

There is no doubt that empowerment comes with waking up physically, and you claim even more power when you exercise the mind and spirit as well. The other authors in this section have addressed many of these approaches, but I would like to especially emphasize three healthy habits. You'll notice the Dalai Lama said, "Wake up." He did not say, "Worry about what you said yesterday or what is going to happen tomorrow." Rather than fret about the things we cannot control, we need to stay present and focus on today, every day.

Kim Kircher uses her professional discipline to concentrate her focus on the present. She survived the threat of losing her husband, first through cancer treatment, then for another 150 days while waiting for a liver donation to save his life. As a paramedic, Kim rescues people stranded on the slopes of Crystal Mountain in Washington, where they strive to get the injured, and often freezing, victim to a transport vehicle in just fifteen minutes. By narrowing their focus to the next fifteen minutes, she and her husband found they could endure his pain, cope with fears of "what if he doesn't get a liver," and manage her type 1 diabetes. Staying in the present, fifteen minutes at a time, helped them survive their ordeal.

Turn on Your Senses

A good way to keep a present focus is to tune in to your senses and notice what they are telling you about your surroundings. How does it feel to touch, smell, taste, and listen to what is happening now? Isn't it amazing how focused and connected that simple exercise makes you feel? While you are at it, notice something beautiful about your surroundings. Feel your heart lift: Your mind is waking up.

Be Grateful

You have surely noticed that whatever you focus on before going to sleep affects your rest and that your thoughts on waking affect your day. If we think about our blessings, whether it is having sweet water to drink or air to breathe, a sisterhood of smart amazing women to enjoy, or being endowed with an ability to create a painting or help another person learn a skill, we free up more zest for our daily activities. Gratitude awakens us; we see our opportunities and rise to our challenges, instead of obsessing about our barriers and failures.

Conquer Fear

Once we wake up and are filled with energy, we are ready to pursue our passion and purpose. The biggest obstacle to achieving our purpose is the fear that we cannot do it. Whether it is lack of self-confidence or overwhelming life circumstances, the real barrier is the fear itself. In the groundbreaking classic, *Feel the Fear . . . and Do It Anyway*, Susan Jeffers, PhD, wrote, "The only way to conquer a fear is to do the very thing we're afraid of." It sounds terrifying, but it works.

It is not easy, though. We are genetically programmed as animals to think of our safety first. That includes meeting our physical needs for shelter and food as well as our emotional needs for love and support. When we face a major change in our lives, like leaving a spouse or starting our own business, we have major fears to overcome. I know you can do it. Think it through. Talk it over with your women friends. I will bet they will have great advice and experiences to share. Plan it out with the best advice you can find. Then do the thing you fear the most.

Find Your Passion and Follow It

Many people live their lives without a thought to pursuing their passion. Work schedules, family routines, annual vacations, and birthdays flow by; the seasons come and go. They are living the life our culture defines as successful, yet they do not feel successful, much less fulfilled. If you recognize this, ask yourself, "What do I love so much that I would do it for free?" When does your heart lift? What makes you smile? Perhaps you love something you are already doing, a hobby or volunteer activity. Take stock of the things that mean the most to you.

Often our passion is born of pain. Rhonda Sciortino has an inspiring story. Abandoned as a baby, she lived in filth and poverty with abusive caregivers. When she was fourteen years old, Rhonda met a teacher who, for the first time in her life, made her feel important. This new feeling of self-worth enabled her to win emancipation from her caregivers at age fifteen. She claimed her power to take responsibility for her own survival and to pursue her passion. Now an adult, she helps children as a national child welfare specialist; she hosts a radio show about overcoming adversity; she wrote a book, *Succeed Because of What You've Been Through*.

Rhonda found her purpose through a traumatic early life, but there are many paths to discovering your passion. After you awaken to the present and act in spite of your fears, your purpose may become apparent. What are your strengths? Do not be shy or a perfectionist about your talent. If you cannot think of anything, ask your women friends who know you better than you know yourself. A life coach or a friend may be able to help unveil your true feelings and skills.

Seize the Opportunity

Once you have identified your purpose, you will notice other women and men who are working to achieve it. Set your intention by articulating a specific goal and time frame. Visualize it as if it has already happened. See yourself in the role you are trying to create. If you have trouble visualizing it, cut pictures from magazines or make drawings yourself for a collage to physically represent your goal. These techniques work. It is a way of involving your entire being in the action of pursuing your passion and purpose.

Celebrate

Once you are there, be sure to recognize your success and congratulate yourself. Women love to do this for others but often shortchange themselves. We barely pause in our momentum as we move on to the next goal. Stop it! Celebrate with your mentor, your network, or a group of sisters; lift each other up and honor your passion and purpose.

A few years ago, I attended a Genshai retreat in California where everyone signed the Book of Greats. I was awed to see my signature among such notables as Mother Teresa and Dr. Viktor Frankl. The point is that each one of us has greatness to share. This experience awakened me to the empowerment of connecting. I also realized that I have a responsibility to live up to my potential. When we help others, we help ourselves.

The empowered women I meet continually inspire me. Every day I exercise my body, mind, and spirit, and pursue my mission of connecting with other women to help them identify their passion and pursue their purpose.

When you are living your passion and achieving your purpose, you will feel more alive and energized than you thought possible.

You will feel the joy and satisfaction of doing something deeply meaningful with your life. Knowing that you are using your gifts to help others and make a positive impact invigorates your whole being.

Are you willing to get started now and use your power to ignite others? Let us connect to create a better world!

Part Three

Connecting to Support Each Other

Women who have claimed their power in the outside world and untangled the webs that block their internal power positively glow with energy and purpose. They are prepared to create a better world and there is no shortage of targets that need improvement. The authors in this third section describe productive ways women can make a difference. The core message among all of them is that each woman needs to support other women everywhere: in her home, workplace, community, nation, and world. No individual woman is as creative, skilled, and powerful as we are together.

The authors in this section will inspire you with their nuts-and-bolts approaches to their philanthropic works. It is not rocket science! Each encountered a problem that touched her soul, and all found ways to provide solutions. These women have found deep satisfaction and meaning in helping others. Wherever your passion lies, reach out to another woman, and make a difference in our world.

Seven Keys to Unlocking Female Leadership

by Janet Rose Wojtalik, EdD
Author, motivational speaker,
and school administrator

*"Give a girl the answer and she will fend for a day.
Give a girl the desire to learn and she will fend for a
lifetime."*

My work began with messages to parents on how to raise strong, resilient, hardy daughters who search for knowledge and have a strong sense of their authentic beauty. As my crusade has grown, my work has broadened to now encompass young women at every age from middle school, to college, to the business world. At the core of my passion is this nagging reality that the glass ceiling, although cracking, still exists. However, also troubling, is that this glass ceiling has a twin and it is within us!

Society works to keep our young women from seeing their true reflection of strength and capability. The messages around us strongly tell us that we are not able, not skilled, not independent, not leadership worthy, and not capable of managing careers and positions that require gumption and strength. This is the more terrifying glass ceiling that is within us. We will not allow ourselves to see our true reflections in that looking glass. Instead, we see someone who is not physically and mentally what society tells us we should be. We see someone who is needy. We see someone who cannot do for herself. We see someone who is afraid.

My message to women everywhere, at every age, is to help each other to see the true beauty and strength within us.

Whether you are a parent, a teacher, a friend, or a boss, you can lift a female to leadership by unlocking those hidden talents and strengths.

We have a responsibility to do all that we can to promote female leadership.

My research has propelled me to develop seven keys that can shape the girls and women in our lives so that they open their minds to their true value, value that unlocks their power and their potential. These seven keys will help them shun those messages that encourage us to measure our worth by our physical beauty and sexuality. These keys will give us a new measuring stick, one that allows our inner strength and beauty to grow. Although it is critical that we begin to shape our girls early, these messages of strength can help us mentor women of all ages.

Branding

The first of these seven keys is the power of branding. What do you think of when you see the word Hershey's? Chocolate, right? How about the word Prada? High-fashion clothes? What about Harley-Davidson? McDonald's? Westinghouse? All of these companies have branded themselves as something. What is your brand? What is your daughter's brand? How are you branding the important females around you? What choices will be made now that will affect your daughter's brand in the future? More importantly, how will she brand herself?

There is an old saying that our children are what we say they are. How do you want to brand your daughter? Do you want to brand her as a princess (who waits for her prince to come and rescue her) or do you want to brand her as a hard worker, or good problem solver, or smart, or willing to try new things? My first key to unlocking leadership is to brand your daughter with words of strength. Take every opportunity you can to notice, to praise, and to strengthen those genuine skills and talents that you want to foster. Tell your daughter she is good at math when she shows success in this area. Encourage this success and then let her know that hard work and determination are her strengths. She will believe you and these traits will grow.

Promote Independence

My second key to unlocking leadership is to promote independence. How many times do you do something for your daughter, just because she is a girl? By not encouraging her to speak up for herself or to solve problems on her own, you are sending her the message that she is not capable of high-level problem solving. Think about the difference in how our sons are managed. We always expect our boys to do for themselves. We train them early that they can and should be independent. On the contrary, we often teach our daughters to be dependent. You can undo those messages. Teach your daughter early that she can do for herself and praise her for her efforts and accomplishments when she does. Also, pay close attention to the messages you send her about your strength. If the message in your home is "Wait until Daddy gets home" to handle a problem, you tell your girls that you are not capable of problem solving on your own. Let her see you make decisions. Encourage her to make her own decisions. Prepare her for adult decision-making and independence.

Promote Thinking

Thirdly, promote thinking. When is the last time you asked your daughter to give her opinion on a world event or situation? Do you engage with her about things that really matter in the world? Do you know her opinion on politics, or poverty, or on the messages today's media send girls about what females should value? Become aware of every teachable moment and engage in thinking conversations with your daughter. Let her know that you know she has opinions and that you value them. Provide her with ideas to consider. Your interest in her and her thoughts will go a long way. What are you planning to buy for your daughter for her next birthday or special holiday? While it may be fun and okay to buy her a doll, a playhouse, or something pink and frilly, how about something that promotes action-based learning and problem solving? Too many times, we fall into the advertiser's trap of what a girl must have. Look at those messages. What are they encouraging our girls to do? I am not saying to avoid those things altogether. What I am saying is to pay attention to what skills those toys foster and choose wisely and diversely.

Promote Learning

Fourth, along with thinking, promote learning. Through your conversations with your daughter, let her know that you value her learning new things. Encourage her to join clubs and activities that will broaden her world. Study and investigate things together. Engage her in talks about world affairs and show her that her thoughts are valued. Encourage her to share with you what she is studying in school. Do not limit her capabilities by not calling attention to them. Support her interest in science and mathematics. We desperately need women in these fields. Take an interest and use her questions or comments for an opportunity to investigate a new area with her. Build her brand in this area. It will go far in developing her into an intelligent, aware, fearless woman.

Promote Authentic Beauty

My fifth key is to promote authentic beauty. If you look at the ads/media around us, all we see are thin, beautiful, fashion-obsessed girls promoting sexuality as a female's true measure of worth. Is that what you want your daughter to value? Or do you want her to value her true inner capabilities and to feel good about her skills and talents? If so, you need to foster those traits. You can do this through your words of support and what you call attention to. Acknowledge her stick-to-it-iveness and her ability to study hard and earn good grades. Let her hear you value those same traits in yourself! If she hears you complaining that your thighs are too big or your waistline too thick, you are sending her the message that you are less because of these physical traits. Do not get me wrong, it is important that you support a healthy body and a healthy mind, but it is the whole package. Promote valuing yourself and your daughter for being the best you both can be!

Promote Education

Sixth, always promote education and let her know she has choices. When I was growing up the message in my home was *when* you go to college and become a teacher, not *if*. That is how we were raised. There was no other option. Be sure your daughter knows that there is an endless array of options for her and do not hold her back by steering her in the direction of typical female fields. Investigate atypical careers. Call her attention to strong women leaders in history, in politics, in your area, and in your family.

If your daughter has a mathematical interest and strength, encourage a career in that area. As I stated earlier we strongly need more women leaders in the fields of science, technology, engineering, and mathematics. Promote education in your home; value it, and your daughter will too!

Talk about what is needed to become successful and independent. Talk about how you value education. Expect her to have skills and marketability.

Promote Awareness

Lastly, but by far not the least important, is to promote awareness. Although movement has occurred to promote equality for women, many obstacles remain. The media continues to portray us as mindless, sexual beings. It is still rare to find women in top leadership positions. There remain many obstacles for women based on false beliefs about what women can and cannot do. It is important that your daughter is aware of these myths and that she has the strength to speak up and stand up for herself. You can help by having conversations with her early about these things. Be aware of the messages you send in your own home. Have you ever heard someone say to a boy, "You throw like a girl"? Has that ever happened in your home? What does that say about girls? That tells me that we cannot be good athletes. Do you agree with that? How about the parent or teacher that says, "She is good at math for a girl"? What does that mean? Girls are not good at math? So many myths exist regarding female capabilities. Your awareness of these negative messages is a giant first step. Help your daughter be aware also. Discuss them. Talk about why they are not true. Find solutions for eliminating them. She will then be armed to resist and undo those messages as she grows into womanhood.

In today's world, our young women are demeaned, bullied, and harassed in subtle ways that often inhibit them from entering into leadership arenas.

It is important that you start conversations early that will encourage your daughter to pay attention to things that make her uncomfortable and to act when that happens. We do not want our girls to accept taking a back seat or being submissive.

What we do want is for our girls to see that glass ceiling and to take action to shatter it, both the one above her head and the one within. We must start today to unlock female strength and to promote female leadership for tomorrow!

You Do Not Have to Be a Feminist to Support Women's Equality

by Cheryl Benton
Founder and publisher of *The Three Tomatoes*

*"Let's not let labels like feminism keep us from focusing
on the issues and working together to create a world
where women and girls are truly equal."*

A few months ago I was invited to the Ms. Foundation's annual Gloria Awards, an inspiring evening that honors amazing women. During the cocktail reception, I found myself face to face with Gloria Steinem herself (who looked dazzling by the way). I introduced myself and suddenly and quite unexpectedly found myself choked with emotion as I thanked her for everything she has done for women. Later that evening and for days to come, I found myself wondering, Where did that come from?

As a woman who came of age in the 1960s, the women's movement unfolded all around me. For much of the 1970s, I wore my blonde hair long and straight and sported aviator glasses, à la Ms. Steinem. However, like many women of my generation, I pursued my education, my career in advertising and marketing, my life as a wife and mother, without ever identifying with a movement, or labeling myself a feminist, thank you very much. I am not alone.

If you ask women if they are advocates or supporters of "social, political, and economic rights and equality for women" (the classic definition of feminism), the overwhelming majority says, "Of course!" Yet, if you ask these same women if they consider themselves "feminists," that is where it starts to get interesting.

Through our website, *The Three Tomatoes*, we recently polled a group of women over the age of forty-five about the term feminism and 71 percent said the term is viewed negatively. An extensive poll conducted by *CBS News* in 2009 on Americans' views on feminism also shows the paradox.

Here are a few of the highlights of that poll:

- While 82 percent of women thought the overall status of women in this country is better than it was twenty-five years ago, and 69 percent of women say the women's movement has made their lives better, 70 percent are reluctant to call themselves feminists.
- Yet, when this definition of a feminist is provided, "A feminist is someone who believes in social, political, and economic equality of the sexes," the majority of women in nearly every demographic group say they are feminist.
- And (this shocked us) Gloria Steinem is unknown to most Americans, including most women. When asked to offer an opinion of her, 78 percent of women were undecided or did not know enough about Ms. Steinem to offer an opinion.

Moreover, American women are not the only ones rejecting the feminist label. The October 2012 issue of *Marie Claire UK* reported that in a poll by Netmums, Britain's largest women's website, only one in seven modern women would call themselves feminists. Age also plays a factor in how women view themselves. Only 9 percent of women aged 25–29 said they identified with the feminist movement, whereas a quarter of women aged 45–50 said they were feminists.

Why Has Feminism Fallen Out of Favor?

First, let's start with the notion of "joining the feminist movement." That has always confused me and I think a lot of other women, too. Where were we supposed to sign up? What was expected of us? If we went to rallies and burned our bras did we get into the feminist club?

Then there is the issue of defining what feminism is. There are so many different schools of feminist thought it makes my head hurt. There is cultural feminism, material feminism, liberal feminism, ecofeminism, and radical feminism, just to name a few.

What about men? The poll numbers reflect even more negatively on feminism when you ask the guys what they think. Many radical feminists exclude men entirely from feminism.

Who "owns" feminism, and who gets to decide if you are in or out? Recently, pop celebrities Katy Perry and Taylor Swift, Yahoo! CEO Marissa Mayer, and former first lady of France, Carla Bruni, were all chastised by feminists for their "ignorance" for publicly saying they do not label themselves as feminists. On the flip side, many prominent feminists were apoplectic when Sarah Palin labeled herself a feminist. Moreover, I am sure there are those reading this essay who will definitely not invite me to the next bra burning.

The term *feminism* was at first a synonym for *femininity* until—near the start of the twentieth century—a newspaper editorial warned about feminists grabbing political power. By now, the term carries so much extraneous baggage it divides rather than unites women, and it distracts them from pursuing their mutual self-interest.

Do We Still Need a Movement for Women's Rights?

Unequivocally, yes, we do need a women's rights movement. Let us go back to that *CBS* poll and one of its findings that really disturbed me. Women were equally divided on whether there is still a need for a strong women's movement. In addition, 45 percent believe that most of the goals of the women's movement have been met.

If that's the case, are the goals of the women's movement met when women in this country still earn only 77 percent of what men earn? Is it acceptable that women make up just 16.6 percent of corporate board officers at *Fortune* 500 companies? That when it comes to women's representation in government, internationally, the United States ranks 71st? Is it acceptable that our Congress debated through two decades before finally passing the Violence Against Women Act (VAWA) in February 2013? Or that the United States is one of seven nations (others include Somalia, Iran, and Sudan) who have yet to ratify the United Nations' women's rights treaty?

While most of us agree that our lives as women in this country are better because of the women's movement, it is not just all about us. Let us talk about the majority of women in the world who are denied education, freedom from violence, economic security, or a voice in their communities. Equality for so many of the world's women remains in the Dark Ages. When thirteen-year-old girls in Afghanistan are shot in the head or have acid thrown in their faces because they want to go to school, when men use the rape of women as a weapon of war, when girls as young as six or seven are forced into marriage, when young girls have their genitalia mutilated, isn't it our moral responsibility to be their voices and stand up for their rights?

If you think women's rights have been achieved, consider these facts from the United Nations, UN Women (the UN's entity for gender equality and the empowerment of women), and the Half the Sky foundation:

- Women comprise 70 percent of the world's poorest people and own only one percent of the titled land.
- Up to 70 percent of women and girls will be beaten, coerced into sex, or otherwise abused in their lifetime.
- Violence against women has become a weapon of war. In Rwanda, up to half a million women were raped during the 1994 genocide.
- One hundred forty million women and girls alive today have undergone female genital mutilation.
- It is estimated that five thousand women are victims of so-called honor killings every year.
- Seventy-five million primary school-age children are not in school. More than half of these children are girls and 75 percent of them live in sub-Saharan Africa and South Asia. Of all the primary-school-age girls globally, 20 percent are not in school.
- One thousand women die from pregnancy or childbirth-related complications globally every day, according to the World Health Organization. That is one every ninety seconds. Some 99 percent of maternal deaths occur in poor countries, particularly in Africa and Asia.

- An estimated 3 million women and girls are enslaved in the sex trade—bought, held, and forced into commercial sex work against their will.

It is clear we still need to fight for the social, political, and economic rights and equality for women and girls everywhere.

Call it what you want, but let us not let words like feminism keep us from focusing on the issues and working together to create a world where women and girls are truly equal—that is a world that will be a much different and better place.

Let us also remember that women's issues are men's issues. We cannot have women's rights without men, so excluding them from our movement will never achieve equality.

It is time to forget the labels that divide us, and focus on the end game—a world where women have equal opportunities and rights and live in a world free from violence and oppression. That is a goal most of us can agree with, yet the biggest threat to women's rights is complacency on the part of many women, and men, too. All this being true, what are some of the things that each of us could do today to make this goal a reality? Here are three ideas:

1. **Become more aware of legislation and how it affects women, for better or worse.** Understand the issues and make your voice heard, especially by your elected representatives.
2. **Use your personal influence and power in your own sphere to champion women and girls in your company, your profession, and your community.** Women need to help other women.
3. **Think globally.** While we have the luxury in this country of debating the issues on equal pay for women, and getting more women in the C-suite and into high-level political offices, there are women in many parts of the world who have few if any rights, and live under oppressive conditions that most of us cannot even imagine. These are women whose voices are not heard, so we must become their voices and provide them with the support they desperately need. Things that happen in distant corners of the world matter to your corner of the world, too.

The central moral challenge of our time is oppression against women and girls, write journalists Nicholas Kristof and Sheryl WuDunn in their acclaimed bestselling book, *Half the Sky: Turning Oppression into Opportunity for Women Worldwide.* I believe it is reaching a tipping point. Oppression is being confronted head-on and change is happening. The authors have been inspired to start a powerful Half the Sky Movement.

Many global organizations work on these issues. UN Women (the *only* entity at the United Nations focused exclusively on women's equality and empowerment) is an organization that I support through the U.S. National Committee for UN Women. Other groups include Women for Women International, and Women's World Banking. Visit the *www.halftheskymovement*

.*org* website and learn more about the issues and the many organizations that are working for change.

Back to Gloria

I think the reason I got so emotional meeting Gloria Steinem was my realization that much of where I am today (along with many other women of my generation) is that she (and others) fought for our equality and rights. We owe her a huge debt of gratitude. While we may not have labeled ourselves feminists, or marched on Washington, or burned our bras, or organized rallies, we heard you and the world heard you. Thank you for letting us stand on your shoulders.

Redefining Sex and Power: How Women Can Bankroll Change and Fund Their Future

by Joanna L. Krotz
Journalist and entrepreneur

"Many women still view philanthropy as a man's game, even though women typically give more than men."

Put women and money in a room—or even in the same sentence—and, inevitably, you can see the sparks fly. This relatively new coupling is throwing off serious heat, fueling transformations large and small from coast to coast, and revolutionizing women's futures.

Even so, issues thrown up by the changing perceptions of sex, money, and power are deep, wide, and ubiquitous. They encapsulate women's shared cultural and sociological influences as well as their uniquely individual psychological makeups.

Whether among women with old wealth, women living paycheck to paycheck, or women in between, I have seen that only after arriving at a clear understanding of emotions about money can you attain the freedom to pursue power. Coming to terms with money fears and feelings, owning and accepting and, yes, sometimes changing, your money personality, will lead to more authentic and effective choices. It will free you from denial, from running away, from giving over to a guy or a relative, and from making decisions by default. "If we don't believe that money gives us voice and power, then we can't use it in a mature way," says a wealth manager who specializes in advising women.

So let us take the journey. Let us dive into the deep pool of women's money dreams, fears, and expectations.

The Elephant in the Room of Women's Financial Empowerment

Workshops and courses designed to teach women about money matters have become quite the rage. Invariably, the focus at such events is on transactions—not transcendence. On spreadsheets—not spreading your wings.

A financial pro, often a guy, holds forth on, say, how to create a budget, the magic of compound interest or choosing a financial planner. You get some handsome marketing materials from the event's sponsoring firm and that is the show.

Such approaches rarely hit women's screens. Women tend to avoid money management and the transactional side of finances until and unless they explore and accept the nature of their emotional engagement with money. How often have you heard a woman say, "I don't do math"?

Research reveals—surprise, surprise—that women and men do not think, talk, behave, or handle money in the same ways. For instance, women tend to see money as a pool that can be drained and run dry. Men tend to see money as a spigot, a faucet they can control and turn off and on to get more. That is not entirely unreasonable when you remember that women, on average, earn less than men throughout their lives and are at greater risk for outliving their savings.

Men also are better at taking risks with money. Women play it safer, and since reward follows risk, it is something women usually need to work on. However, women typically do better in investments because they kick tires, do homework, make choices, and then stay the course. Men tend to be all about winning and grabbing the brass ring. So, men move in and out of investments to score or make a killing while women work to achieve goals such as the kid's college tuition. Women tend to be more patient.

What Is Your Money For?

None of this is to suggest that financial playbooks are not important. Refusing to learn how to manage your money can cost you, perhaps dearly. However, you can easily find dozens of pros and planners to work with you on conventional financial lessons, not to mention access to all the books and online resources around. What is missing and all too rare in financial literacy seminars is even a hint of discussion about the complex feelings money evokes or the purpose behind investments and money management. That goes for men as well as women. What, after all, is money for? What kind of future or legacy do you wish to shape? Why do the workshops never address the values we bring to money management?

People often avoid financial planning because they think talking about far-reaching decisions will lock them in. In fact, it is typically just the reverse.

Planning and managing your money lets you fund your beliefs, passions, and legacy.

As one family wealth consultant puts it: "Fifty or sixty years from now, what would you like to say about your family and dreams. If you want your family close, productive, accepting diversity, making a difference in the world, then what are you going to do now to get you there?"

Stories about women who are committing to a bigger purpose, to building something that will outlive them, are surfacing frequently, especially as boomer women consider what is next. These are altogether contemporary legacies, on a scale without precedent. Many such examples are ongoing and under the radar, since few media outlets are reporting on women's local or individual philanthropy.

In sum, how about building a bridge from the constant striving for more to the blissful feeling that you have enough?

Financial Security Does Not Equal Emotional Security

Most of us are taught to think that sudden wealth is a huge stroke of luck, especially women, who are socialized to view money as security and the route to happiness, as in the Cinderella fable. However, achieving sudden wealth is often far from the all-purpose enabler people imagine. Money can often be immobilizing.

We have all heard sad tales about lottery winners who end up destroyed because the money overwhelms their lives. Until such instant millionaires feel in control of their newfound windfall and, in many cases, discover the rewards of purpose and giving, they frequently feel burdened and unable to enjoy their good fortune.

Paralyzing feelings of guilt and financial approach or avoidance can happen at any point along the money trail, even for those who grow up wealthy, when you'd imagine the mantle of money would be settled and comfortable. For example, that is what happened to one young heiress, now in her mid-fifties, who came into money when her mother died, leaving her a substantial inheritance. She was only eighteen.

When I talked to her, decades later, her emotions were still palpable. She felt she didn't deserve the money. She had grown up knowing her family was well off, of course, but the depth of that privilege did not really hit her until she came into the fortune. She saw how much other people had to struggle while she did not, especially the group of young artists who were then her friends. She did not tell them or, in fact, anyone about her money, and she didn't date, either.

The money weighed her down and made her guilty. She remained, as she put it, "in the closet," until age thirty-two—fourteen long years later—when she connected with a consultancy that helped her become comfortable with her wealth and guided her to put the money to work for social good. Then she found freedom. Denying money's influence, hiding from its power or pretending that money doesn't make a difference won't get you where you want to go.

Tracking Women's Rising Economic Power

Today, millions of American women have achieved what is called "independent means."

You cannot look into women's love/hate relationship with money without acknowledging the recent past. That is, the spectacular rise of women's social and economic power over the past half-century. Women alive today belong to the most affluent, educated, and longest-lived generations in history.

The latest IRS figures report that 43 percent of the nation's 2.7 million top wealth holders are women (top wealth is defined as having $1.5 million or more in assets without home equity). Assets of those more than 1 million women are valued at over $5 trillion, or about 42 percent of the $12 trillion total holdings of top wealth holders. Not surprisingly, more than a third (35 percent) of those women are older, age 50–65.

In addition, women control nearly half of estates worth more than $5 million. They account for more than 80 percent of consumer spending, to the tune of $3.7 trillion. And more than four out of ten privately held businesses—over 8 million U.S. firms—are owned by women, and employ close to 8 million people and generate about $1 trillion in revenue. In addition, for the first time in the nation's history, partly owing to the recession, women now hold a majority of the nation's jobs.

At the upper end, women now surpass men in educational achievement. The U.S. Department of Education estimates that for every 100 male college graduates in 2013, there were 140 women grads. Women have earned 9.2 million more degrees than men in the past three decades. Women also are enrolling in postgraduate and MBA programs in record numbers. In the United States, women have a nearly three-to-two majority in graduate education and, in 2010, for the first time, more women than men earned doctoral degrees.

Even more interesting, in 2010, women outearned their husbands in about a quarter of households with spouses eighteen to sixty-five years of age. Traditional models truly are being revised, however, change can be slow. Surveys found that marriage rates tended to drop among the couples where the wife could potentially outearn her husband. It would seem it's still not socially acceptable for women to earn more than their men do. Then there's women's longevity compared to men. On average, women live about five years longer than men do. They tend to marry men older than themselves and they remarry less frequently than men do after a spouse dies. All in all, women aged sixty-five and older are now three times more likely to be widowed than their male counterparts.

Translating Economic Might Into Political Muscle

All of this puts more and more women in line to control inherited money from husbands and families. Of course, with more education and leadership positions in business, they are also earning significant income themselves.

With this growing earning power, expanding professional skills, profitable businesses of their own, and deepening control over family trusts and inheritances, women increasingly have the wherewithal to demand a seat at the tables of policy and power.

Yet, we do not see that. Women are not moving into the halls of political power at nearly the accelerated rate at which they are gaining more financial independence. The 2012 elections sent historic numbers of women to Congress, but what does that actually add up to?

Sadly, the total is a scant 101 women out of 535 members of Congress. That is only 81 women out of 435 representatives and twenty women out of 100 senators. Do not forget women now account for 51 percent of the U.S. population. Who represents us? Consider those congressional hearings on reproductive rights in 2012 that consisted of all-male committees and experts.

Part Three: Connecting to Support Each Other | 163

Where are the people making law and policy that understand women's lives, needs, and rights?

The 2013 congressional hearings into sexual assault in the military provide even more pointed lessons. Outraged women legislators, new to the Senate Armed Services Committee, dubbed "one of the Senate's most testosterone-driven panels" by the *New York Times*, forced the public hearings. There are two lessons to be drawn from this:

1. When women get seats at the table, the agenda and priorities shift. But in the end, the committee's senior male leadership refused to budge on the critical chain-of-command issue, which means thousands of assault victims still have no recourse but to report abuse to their abusers—hardly an option.
2. We need more women in positions of power.

Research tells us that both male and female voters are much more judgmental about the appearance and style of a female candidate than of a male candidate. Although all candidates are judged on looks to some degree, women have an uphill battle in persuading voters to judge them on their merits rather than their appearance.

In fact, despite those impressive advances and statistics, there is scarce mainstream acknowledgement of women's ever-growing assets and power. Self-made billionaires like Michael Bloomberg or Bill Gates are seen as smart, strategic, accomplished, and enviable. Women with wealth? Not so much. When women of means step into the limelight, they're frequently dismissed or deconstructed, labeled greedy, indulgent, stupid, bitchy, gold diggers, anything but powerful and admirable.

Money continues to carry a serious gender bias. Women have only lately begun to earn significant dollars, reach the top of professional ladders, and control the fortunes that men have traditionally managed. Around the country, the larger society continues to be tough on women of wealth and power. Therefore, unlike men, women do not gain as much from promoting their status and power. Neither men nor women are entirely comfortable with women in charge.

No wonder, then, that however high women jump to clear the hurdles and move into male domains, visceral messages—from the media, from bosses, from childhood, from other family members—do drag them down. Women still are not supposed to concern themselves with money.

Finding Your Money Personality

I am sure you have heard many times before that the traditional male values that money implies, including independence, power, status, and financial reward, constitute the final frontier for women. However, old habits are dying very hard. Think about it. When you pick up the check for guys, how do you feel? What happens when you meet men who earn considerably less than you do?

As a result, women often hand over the power that money confers to others, usually men, whether lovers, husbands, or professional advisers. That way, we can feel cared for, safe, and feminine.

This is not easy stuff to change or adopt. That is because money and means, of course, are not merely the paper stuff we use to buy and sell things. Money also represents the emotions and values that we learn from our families and our circumstances, which we internalize.

We all bring individual agendas, histories, fantasies, expectations, and anxieties to our financial transactions—to spending and saving as much as to giving and investing. Our money personality comes from an array of influences, from individual experiences as we grow up to the culture's loud voice about taboos and appropriate behavior for women.

Yet, as we have seen, lots more women are coming into more and more money, frequently from a sudden event such as selling a business, or receiving an inheritance or a divorce settlement. That means many more women must come to terms with the meaning of financial success. The solution is to do the personal work of defining your relationship toward money and its role in your life.

New York psychologist Annette Lieberman, who works mostly with women artists, says: "We can't handle money responsibly until we understand what money means psychologically."

Some years ago, after noticing that her women clients were increasingly bringing issues of money into their sessions, Lieberman conducted a study of women and their money attitudes. That uncovered what she calls, "deadly symptoms of money phobia for women." The personalities that emerged from her in-depth study include:

- Money Blind women, who close their eyes and think of money as vague or unreal
- Money Squeamish women, who find the desire for money greedy or vulgar
- Money Deniers, who wait for someone or something to rescue them
- Money Eluders, who want to make more money but are paralyzed by anxieties they will not define
- Money Folly victims, who solve emotional conflicts with excessive spending or what we have come to call "retail therapy"
- Money Paranoid women, who use their money as a fortress to keep themselves protected and insulated

Hit any nerves for you? The key here is that money decisions are emotionally based.

Flexing the Power of One

We are still living with the stereotypes of sex roles. Men go off, have adventures, and unearth treasures. Women, however much they protest, often suffer from the Prince Charming syndrome, waiting for the hero to guide their future.

> As women, we must reject that idea that only a man can provide for our security. We must find the will and the comfort level to use our money and resources for choices that have meaning for us.

Dr. Astrid Heger did. In 1983, as a young resident pediatrician in Los Angeles, Heger volunteered at the local hospital. It may seem unthinkable today, but back then, children who had been sexually abused were physically examined not once but repeatedly and routinely so medical and legal experts could testify about the injuries at multiple court hearings.

Heger was outraged to learn of such unnecessary added trauma. She also was indignant about the lack of objectively documented evidence, which meant every case hinged on someone's subjective opinion of abuse.

Thus Heger pioneered the use of video documentation and created rigorous methods of evaluation so kids would be physically examined only once and the courts would have access to fact-based legal evidence. Then she launched a one-woman campaign, first getting a law passed in California that admitted video documentation as legal evidence in court. With that precedent, she mounted a campaign that passed similar laws in every state in the nation. Kids today no longer have to go through what Heger witnessed in 1983.

By looking into what drives your financial habits and choices, you will be able to take charge and express your true values and beliefs. You will experience your power.

Outrage galvanized young Dr. Heger. Although she had no financial backing, she followed her heart and her head, trusting that support would follow. With only a trickle of funding and no salary or staff, Heger began treating vulnerable children in a temporary clinic she founded, actually an abandoned trailer parked on the hospital's parking lot. Authorities kept warning her off. But over the years, social workers, counselors, and police officers kept bringing her more and more victims of family violence because they had nowhere else to take the kids.

Eventually, Heger's programs officially became the LAC + USC Medical Center's Violence Intervention Program (VIP), which went on to raise $2 million and move into a renovated facility. Nowadays, with an operating budget of upward of $11 million, VIP is a one-stop care center that annually evaluates more than 20,000 victims of family violence, sexual assault, and abuse.

Astrid Heger's tenacity and full embrace of her passion serves as a reminder that each of us can make a difference. Each of us embodies the Power of One.

African Women Rising—
Empowering the Agents of Change

by Rebecca Tinsley
Founder of Waging Peace

*"Our role must be to identify the women
who are bringing about local change,
and then to support them."*

Barbara is a psychotherapist from Minnesota. Twice a year this sixty-four-year-old grandmother travels to a remote village in northern Uganda where there is neither electricity nor running water. For three weeks at a time, she teaches former child soldiers, all of them damaged by the brutality they endured and the violence they were forced to inflict on others. Once Barbara has trained them to manage their own trauma, she prepares them to help others who have survived the same horrors at the hands of Joseph Kony's notorious Lord's Resistance Army (LRA).

When I first visited northern Uganda in 2008, a few months after the LRA had retreated, I found an area devastated by twenty-two years of war. I assumed the best thing my charity, Network for Africa, could do was provide a school. Then I listened as local women told me how they were affected by the violence: most had bullet scars and had lost loved ones; many had been raped, and almost all had witnessed atrocities. How could people rebuild their lives when they were so psychologically scarred?

When we did a survey, we found 40 percent of women considered suicide at least weekly, so traumatized were they by their experiences. They needed to manage their post-traumatic stress before they could learn improved agricultural techniques or form business cooperatives. That was when I called Barbara in Minnesota.

Within a week of Barbara's arrival, women told her that, thanks to her training, they had enjoyed the first decent night's sleep in a decade. Soon we had hundreds of participants in Barbara's classes. The most able students became volunteer counselors, and, equipped with bikes provided by our donors, they now visit outlying villages, teaching others how to manage their trauma through visualization therapy and breathing exercises.

Having established our network of counselors-on-bikes, we added messages about HIV mitigation, domestic violence, substance abuse, savings and loan schemes, and family planning. Our former child soldiers are now trusted pillars of the community, imparting much-needed information to thousands of people. Once they have helped people manage their trauma, they train and support them in rebuilding their war-torn livelihoods.

In addition, because they are local, rather than exotic Western development "experts," they have a credibility that outsiders will never attain. They are also role models, inspiring others facing similar challenges to become leaders.

The main beneficiaries of this remarkable project are women, who carry the greatest burden in a post-conflict society. In modern war, women are deliberately targeted for systematic rape and abuse, because by destroying the will of women, you shatter their society.

By the same measure, if you wish a community to recover and rebuild, you must empower the women and girls, because it is on their shoulders that responsibility rests. In much of Africa, women do all domestic work (without electricity or running water or labor-saving appliances), all agricultural work, and they care for the young, the sick, and the elderly. In refugee camps around the world, it is the women who hold families together, getting everyone up in the morning, facing each day with as much optimism and sense of purpose as they can muster.

We in the developed world must therefore have the humility to listen to African women: just because someone is illiterate, it does not mean she is stupid. It simply means she did not have the chance to go to school. She usually knows what solutions work best, and they tend to be uncomplicated ideas, rather than the grand schemes favored by government officials.

For instance, giving women mosquito nets, and training them to use them, has an enormous impact on cutting child mortality. Providing clean water and first-aid training means millions of babies will survive childhood. Teaching women to read and write means they can no longer be exploited with such ease by employers or shopkeepers. Giving a woman a goat or a chicken provides her with a source of protein for her family and a potential business.

We, as concerned women in the developed world, have a profound impact when we bring in specialists to train African women who then pass on the skills to people in their communities. In the process, we create enlightened agents of change. These local women have a greater chance of success than the utterly alien white persons who come to Africa with the best intentions, doing a job that an African could do, such as helping build an orphanage. The fundamental question remains: for whose benefit is this project? Is it to make an American volunteer feel better about herself, or to empower an African woman to play a greater role in her male-dominated society?

The more rural and traditional a society is, the harder it is for change to occur. Let us dispense with the politically correct nonsense about respecting the cruel and harmful African practices that make women's lives so miserable. Given a chance, women want the same opportunities to fulfill their potential that we take for granted. They want their daughters to have the schooling they were denied. Hence, Westerners who defer to tradition because they are terrified of causing offence or appearing colonialist are part of the problem, not the solution.

By failing to confront the imbalance of power that burdens women so unfairly, we guarantee that Africa will not prosper. Some visitors from our comparatively privileged world have a romantic vision of life in rural Africa. They are charmed when they see fields of women with babies tied to their backs, tending their crops without any mechanical help, working under a burning sun without a drink of water all day.

Those women are unlikely to see the fruit of their labors because the men in their lives (husbands, fathers, brothers) decide how it is spent. If the women are unlucky, the proceeds will buy alcohol or sex with someone who may be HIV positive. Many girls will have no say in whom they marry and little chance to go to school. Although they have rights under their country's constitution, they will never know about those laws because they are illiterate, and the men in their lives are unlikely to enlighten them.

They often have no choice when they have intercourse, and no chance to plan their families. They may be under pressure to produce a child each year because men want to be seen as virile. With no clinic nearby, they will lose several babies to medical ailments that are easily resolved in the West. They will be wary when they become pregnant because in some parts of

Africa a woman has a one-in-seven lifetime chance of dying in pregnancy or childbirth (the comparable figure in Ireland is one in forty-two thousand). They will nurse family members through preventable but debilitating illnesses. Resourceful and resilient as they are, they will struggle to make ends meet. They will be exhausted by the age of twenty-five.

Our role must be to identify the women who are bringing about local change, and then to support them. The credibility of the messenger is vital. For instance, five years ago in Rwanda I met Peace who used her spare time after work each day to train the poor, illiterate genocide survivors in her neighborhood. Sitting on her veranda, women gathered to hear Peace talk about their legal rights, family planning, nutrition, hygiene, domestic violence, and HIV. Soon she had three hundred women in her yard, desperate to learn how to improve their life chances.

With our help, Peace now has a center running courses in literacy, health, first aid, HIV mitigation, cooking, and hygiene. Local experts train women in hairdressing and handicrafts so they have a source of income. With the help of Rwandan voluntary groups, Peace involves women and their partners in learning about the legal rights of women and children, and about family planning. As she says, unless we bring the men along, we will not change much.

One of Peace's "graduates" is Joan, a survivor of unmentionable horrors during the genocide. Joan was illiterate and desperately poor, even by African standards, when she arrived at Peace's center. Now Joan can read and write, and is in a business cooperative. With her newly found confidence, Joan has been elected to the local council and represents her part of town. Her journey was unimaginable three years ago; now she is a leader who has discovered her voice.

Another of Peace's graduates is Francoise. Like the others in her cooperative, her priority is to educate and feed her children, to break the cycle of poverty blighting Africa. "I am also proud of myself," she says. "There is now always food on the table. This group, working together, has helped me so much and they are my friends—not just business partners. Now that I am earning money even the shopkeepers have confidence in me. They will give me credit and know that I will pay it back. I have respect in the community. They say 'those are the working women.'"

Joan, Peace, and Francoise are some of the reasons that Africa has a brighter future than ever before.

The role of relatively prosperous women in the developed world is to empower women in developing countries.

When I ask the women in our training projects what they value most, they never fail to knock me flat when they say: "Here I have found friends, and we help each other. And when women in your country support us, we know you believe in us and care about us. We know you love us."

Information:
The Best Form of Philanthropy

by Shirley Osborne
CEO of Posh Affairs, Inc.

*"Women all over the world are moving to autonomy
and self-determination."*

There was a man named John Simmons who, in mid-nineteenth-century Boston, around the time of the American Civil War and during one of the most intense periods of mass immigration into America, owned one of the largest garment manufacturing businesses in the United States. The overwhelming majority of his factory workers were women, in his case, specifically, war widows, unmarried young women, and immigrant women who had left their home countries in Europe, and in lesser numbers, Asia. These women were hoping for respite from social ills that included economic hardship, famine, and religious and ethnic persecution.

Most of these women knew little English, or none at all, and indeed many were illiterate even in their native languages. They had very little sophistication in any area. John Simmons knew the difficulties that this lack of knowledge occasioned them, and he was well aware of the exploitation and abuse to which it rendered them vulnerable. He knew how difficult, if not altogether impossible, it would be for them to participate fully in the systems of their new country, gain access to vital services and support, and adequately safeguard themselves and their families, with so little knowledge of the American language.

These women had come to America seeking better prospects for their lives and livelihoods, and less-deprived circumstances for their families, but the living conditions in which they found themselves in their new country were saturated with poverty, abuse, disease, crime, and social marginalization. The social mobility they craved was mostly elusive. It was difficult for them to find their way through the maze of bureaucracy that surrounded opportunities even to get charity, and in many instances they were subjected to institutionalized discrimination and systemic marginalization.

Simmons was aware of the community violence and domestic abuse to which so many of his workers fell victim, partly because of current attitudes toward women, prevailing notions of women's place in society and homes, and discrimination against their ethnicities. In no small part because they had so little information at their disposal, these women could not advocate for themselves in any meaningful way.

He knew that these women stood little chance of improving their lot in life—the major reason the immigrant women had journeyed to America in the first place—unless they were able to access and utilize information. Therefore, he brought teachers into his factories to instruct his workers in reading and writing in the English language, among other things. When these women finished working in the evenings, they took classes, right there at their sewing machines.

When John Simmons died in Boston, Massachusetts, on August 29, 1870, he left in his will provisions for his estate to "found and endow an institution to be called Simmons Female

College, for the purpose of teaching medicine, music, drawing, designing, telegraphy, and other branches of art, science, and industry best calculated to enable the scholars to acquire an independent livelihood."

In 1973, Drs. Margaret Hennig and Anne Jardim presented a plan to Simmons College for a new kind of MBA, and in 1975, the college instituted the first Master of Business Administration designed specifically for women's career and leadership success. Nowadays, Simmons MBA classes are attended by women from all over the world, who are being educated for power and principled leadership, and who are advancing John Simmons's commitment to women's empowerment and prospects for self-determination far outside of Boston, Massachusetts.

My MBA class of '95 included a woman who had grown up in Communist Russia, another from the very newly democratic Republic of South Africa, and me, born and reared on one of the very smallest islands in the Caribbean. An Indian classmate gave us an inside look, relating firsthand experiences of how a woman goes about building a relationship and maintaining a family when her marriage has been arranged by her parents with no requirement for her consent. There was a German woman who worked for BMW, the much-desired luxury car that sells itself as "the ultimate driving machine," and a woman of Chinese heritage who copied pages from her classmates' textbooks, because she was taking classes without her husband's full knowledge, and those large and numerous textbooks that were required reading would have given her away at home.

The philanthropy of one man, his patronage in an era when women in the United States were not enfranchised, his compassion and far-sightedness in the days long before *Roe v. Wade* and Title IX, resonates still, today, and affects lives far from the shores of the United States. This, he effected at a time when very few women had either the money or the power to practice this level of philanthropy. One hundred and fifty years later, many women all over the world have this level of wealth and power.

It is up to women, then, as we advance in the power structures and economic institutions of the world, no matter how we acquire that advancement, to reach back, reach down, reach out, and embrace other women, pull them in, give them a hand up.

It is incumbent upon women that, as we become more powerful and rich, with greater access to avenues of power and sources of wealth both traditional and novel, we remain particularly mindful of the gaps in equity that persist both between women and men, and among women in all the various regions of the world. We must actively seek the elimination of the disparities and injustices that hold women back, and which as a direct consequence, restrict the well-being of our families and hinder the development of our societies.

The philanthropy that has been, and will continue to be, vital to women's continued empowerment can be conducted in any of a million different ways. However, it is my submission that the best, most sustainable forms of philanthropy that will have the biggest, most enduring impact are to give women information, to facilitate their access to sources of information, and to support them in acquiring the skills with which to utilize and benefit from information. History bears this out.

Many women are indeed focusing their philanthropic efforts onto this exact sphere, no matter how they came by the means with which to engage in philanthropy. Among them are the four whom I mention here, who have acquired their wealth through traditional avenues such as marriage and inheritance, or earned it through their own business acumen. Each of them deliberately, and with clear intent, eschews the conventional methods of helping others, and seeks creative, collaborative ways of supporting people by informing them rather than giving charitable handouts.

Wallis Annenberg is the daughter of a very wealthy man, a public benefactor of immense significance in twentieth century California. Through The Annenberg Foundation, Wallis carries on her father's legacy, advancing public well-being by funding community education, PBS programs, and innovative projects that seek to shift and open up people's perspectives on the world in which they participate.

Such was the motivation for the community Universally Accessible Treehouse, which she commissioned for Torrance, California, and the Annenberg School for Communication and Journalism at the University of Southern California, which is described as a center for inquiry and dialogue among scholars and professionals in communication, journalism, public policy, media, and education. Through the Annenberg Foundation, she makes funding available to the Harlem Children's Zone, which provides free support for children and families in Harlem, New York, in the form of parenting workshops, a preschool program, and three public charter schools.

Melinda French married Bill Gates in 1994, and soon thereafter, cofounded the Bill & Melinda Gates Foundation. Not surprisingly, given the nature of the commercial activity that makes her philanthropy possible, much of the attention of her foundation focuses on facilitating people's access to information. The mission of the foundation's United States Program is to help ensure greater opportunity for all Americans through the attainment of secondary and post-secondary education. It regularly makes grants in support of free public access to computers and the Internet through local public libraries.

Reputed to be the largest transparently operated private foundation in the world, with an endowment in excess of $36 billion, the Bill & Melinda Gates Foundation underwrites a Global Development Program that seeks to increase opportunities for people in developing countries. It aims to overcome hunger and poverty through narrowing the digital divide in the United States and many developing countries around the world, and to combat infectious diseases by, among other things, "closing gaps in knowledge and science and creating critical platform technologies in areas where current tools are lacking."

Oprah Winfrey is a self-made media mogul who has dominated the television screens in the United States for much of the past twenty-five years or so, as an immensely popular and highly respected daytime talk-show host. Through the years, she has attracted attention and viewership for her generosity and largesse, and for initiatives such as her Book Club and her Angel Network. She has been a very vocal and active supporter of education and teachers, and regularly donates large amounts of money for university scholarships and other educational ventures.

In January 2007, she very proudly conducted the opening ceremonies for the Oprah Winfrey Leadership Academy for Girls in South Africa. The academy, supported by Oprah's foundation in Chicago, Illinois, is a free residential school for academically talented girls. Oprah purposefully selects girls who come from disadvantaged families and who, without the academy, would not otherwise have a chance at an education. She says that "the school . . . will train them to become decision-makers and leaders."

Jacqueline Novogratz runs a nonprofit organization that *Forbes* magazine declares is "not a charity." Described as one of the most innovative players shaping philanthropy today, she used her experience in banking, microfinance, and traditional philanthropy to start the Acumen Fund in 2001. Her mission is to create a world beyond poverty through investing in emerging leaders and breakthrough ideas. The organization's vision is a world in which every human being will have access to the critical goods and services they need so that they can make decisions and choices for themselves and unleash their full human potential.

Speaking at the Peterson Institute for International Economics in 2010, then secretary of state Hillary Rodham Clinton, who formalized the concept "women's rights are human rights," reminded her audience of the studies that have shown that when a woman receives even one year of schooling, her children are less likely to die in infancy or suffer from illness or hunger, and more likely to go to school themselves. She also told them, "You know the proverb, 'Give a man a fish and he'll eat for a day, but teach a man to fish and he'll eat for a lifetime'? Well, if you teach a woman to fish, she'll feed the whole village."

Clinton's two statements spell out the reality of societies in every country of our world and underscore the value added when women gain access to information. The United Nations Population Fund articulates the general consensus on its website: "Equality between men and women exists when both sexes are able to share equally in the distribution of power and influence; have equal opportunities for financial independence through work or through setting up businesses; enjoy equal access to education and the opportunity to develop personal ambitions."

Issues respond best, and most lastingly, to action based on knowledge and information. Equality and empowerment depend upon women's access to information; human rights— women's and everyone else's—are at risk when access to information is restricted.

Historical evidence makes it clear that individual quality of life and societal well-being improve measurably and permanently when people are educated and have access to information. The indications are irrefutable that information and education are the most direct, effective, and sustainable routes to women's empowerment and development, and to their power to change the world for the better, which, after all, is the whole point of philanthropy.

Live Your Legacy: Leadership, Philanthropy, and Transformation

by Aurea McGarry
Emmy Winning TV Show Host, Creator, and
Executive Producer of the *Live Your Legacy* TV
series, and the founder and host of Live Your
Legacy Summit

*"Look closely into what your life has been so far and
what you could turn into your legacy."*

I was born to a Camelot life. My father named me Aurea, which means beautiful in Greek. That describes how I began my life. I had everything a little girl could ask for. My mother was gorgeous. She had been a model for commercials and *Cosmopolitan*. Her beauty was only exceeded by her love. She loved us more than anything and was funny and supportive for all three of her children. I was the baby of the family. My father was a first-generation immigrant who traveled from Greece to Ellis Island with his parents. He worked hard to achieve the American dream. He became an accomplished Harvard graduate who spoke Greek, English, and Latin. He made millions in the stock market and literally became a multimillionaire Greek tycoon.

Of course, I went to the best private schools in New York City, lived on Park Avenue, then 86th Street. Summer vacations were the stuff dreams are made of. We spent three months at Lake Placid every year where I skated in ice-skating shows with future Olympic stars such as Dorothy Hamill, Janet Lynn, and Dick Button. I glided blissfully through life held aloft on a silver platter.

This all came crashing down when I turned fifteen. My father was brutally murdered gangland style, shot three times in the head and thrown out of his car onto the side of the road where two hitchhikers found him. My Camelot lifestyle dissolved forever. It left us broke overnight and living in a roach-infested apartment in Queens. That is when I began to learn how to survive and even thrive in spite of—or perhaps because of—what happened in my life. Mom found work at a law firm, and I walked dogs in my previous 86th Street neighborhood and babysat. My brother and sister moved out, but, together, Mom and I worked our way back to Manhattan in only six months.

Even though we were back on the upswing from the loss of my father, life was different. Things were no longer handed to me on a silver platter. However, I had been blessed with a positive attitude and willingness to adapt to a different lifestyle. Perhaps it was because I was young and had the emotional support of a loving mother, but I still felt fortunate and remained positive as I waitressed to earn enough money to go to school and study acting, theater, and dance. Then I moved to Florida to go to college and pursued different jobs and ultimately a home-based cosmetic business. I found God and developed a strong reliant faith that gave me more survival skills. In fact, I felt blessed, successful, and happy.

Part of my very strong faith is a firm belief that everything that happens to you in life has a purpose, and God can turn it all around to good if you allow it. My life's struggles might have stopped many people. If you perceive difficult events in life as negative and yourself as a victim of circumstances, it can trap you in a prison of fear and make you unable to move forward. With my faith and the support of people who loved me, I refused to let it stop me. In fact, I always believed that whatever was happening had a good reason, even when I had no idea at the time what that reason could possibly be.

In Florida, I met and married a pastor's son. I thought, since he was a pastor's son, we would have the ideal life together, but that was not the case. After seven years of trying to cope with ongoing abuse, I finally escaped with my four-year-old daughter. The support of my mom, stepfather, and my home-based business friends made it possible. As happens with many women who try to end an abusive relationship, my ex-husband stalked me for years.

Shortly after my escape, my mother was diagnosed with liver and lung cancer. I lost her (my first best friend) only five months after we found out she was sick. It almost killed me, too. I felt so lost and alone I might really have died, but for Brian, the love of my life, who I met just three months before she died. I felt that God knew what I needed and put Brian in my life to help me go on. Although it was extremely hard to lose my mom, Brian (my prince) made it possible to smile again.

After marrying Brian, life was good. I was enjoying huge success in my home-based business and at the top of my game on a national level. My then-thirteen-year-old daughter was thriving, too. Not for long, however, as my next hurdle would completely change my life, shape my future, and be the birth of my life's legacy.

Three years into my new incredibly happy marriage, I was diagnosed with non-Hodgkin lymphoma on my thirty-eighth birthday in 1999. Doctors conducted emergency surgery and found my chest cavity full of cancer. Fortunately, it had not metastasized, but it was lying on top of many of my organs.

They removed *everything* it was touching, including half of my left lung, part of my right lung, my thymus, and the lining around my heart. They disconnected half my diaphragm and removed the left thoracic nerve to my vocal cord. First, they gave me the bad news: speaking above a very faint whisper would be impossible from this day forward. Then they gave me the good news: my cancer was curable and after chemo I would be fine. They were right. I have been cancer-free ever since my last chemo treatment in February 2000. Then God stepped in and healed my voice. Everyone, even the doctors, say it was a miracle. My story was even featured on *The 700 Club* TV show.

Since I am convinced that everything happens for a reason, I have not wasted this second chance. I have become not merely a survivor but a *sur-thriver*! I developed a burning desire to use my voice and create a legacy of what I will have accomplished in my life, of what I would pass on to others, and for what I would be remembered. Not only am I talking but I have talked for a living ever since. I am determined to use this most precious gift for good. I produced and hosted a PBS television show called *Live Your Legacy*, to tell the stories about people who were using their talents and passion to make the world a better place. I won an Emmy award for the episode about Noah's Ark Animal Sanctuary in Locust Grove, Georgia. The episode featured an amazing woman, Jama Hedgecoth, who has rescued over 1,800 animals and raised over 305 foster children to date. Her legacy is inspiration for all of us to use our talents to help create good in the world for others.

In 2011, after twenty-two *Live Your Legacy* episodes about similarly inspiring people, I transformed the TV show into my biggest passion and what I see as my own life's purpose: to help other people live their legacy. The national live event series is called "Live Your Legacy Summit." The summit is an exciting one-day event that brings nonprofit organizations together with new supporters. I firmly believe that everyone has a legacy. They may not have discovered it yet, or they may doubt their ability to make it happen. Each summit's goal is to help people dissolve their doubts and turn their dreams into their life's legacy and a fulfilling success.

Entrepreneurs of both new businesses and charities attend the summit to get help in identifying and designing their legacies. Mornings are spent getting acquainted with the national speakers who introduce their expertise and present an overview of various aspects of entrepreneurship: overcoming obstacles, getting exposure through public relations and social media, acquiring and managing finances, and running a home-based business, to name a few. Afternoons are spent in mastermind sessions. These longer breakout sessions allow attendees to target specific areas of interest and need, and to get vital information about how to get their legacy underway or proceed in a different direction, improve effectiveness, change their scope, and advance their passion in ways to guarantee success.

Summit evenings are the most exciting part of the day. A special celebration honors the heroes who are living their legacies and making an impact on the world. These outstanding people are nominated before the event. The winners are awarded gifts from sponsors, plaques and recognition, and a posting on the *http://LiveYourLegacySummit.com* website. Sometimes unforeseen rewards are also presented. When Haley Kilpatrick, founder of Girl Talk, a girl-to-girl mentoring program for middle-school girls, became a Living Legend Honoree, a corporate business vendor in attendance donated $18,000 to Haley's foundation. This spontaneous gift is just one example of how the summits can be important turning points for those who attend, not only through what they learn, but also from the networking and support they provide for each other.

The Living Legend Honorees are the true heroes, and they need to be acknowledged and celebrated. I believe there are more good people on this earth doing good things for others and making this world a better place than bad people doing destructive acts of violence. They just do not get the same amount of media attention. I am on a mission to change that. Because of all I have been through, and especially nearly losing my voice, I feel compelled to use it in the service of these heroes who dedicate their lives to philanthropic work.

Since the inaugural event on September 10, 2011, five Live Your Legacy Summits have honored seventeen Legacy Honorees including Justin Biebers' vocal coach, Jan Smith; female race car driver, Shea Holbrook; and Mrs. World, April Lufriu, who all live their life with huge passions for their charities and to do good. These purposeful and powerful Live Your Legacy Summits continue to grow with the goal of making them as big an influence and help to nonprofits as Oprah was to books and their authors. At our website people can nominate their favorite heroes for a chance to be honored for their philanthropy.

Because of hard times, not good times, I have found my purpose, passion, and life's work. I have my voice back for a reason, and I am going to use it for good in the biggest and best ways possible.

I encourage everyone to look closely into what your life has been so far and what you could turn into a legacy so powerful that

it could live on and create good in the world long after you are gone.

One of my favorite quotes is "When I die, I want to be totally used up without any talent or gifts left unused." God has given us all everything we need to accomplish our legacy and it is our job to find it among chaotic circumstances. When you encounter an obstacle, go over it, under it, around it, or through it. Being rolled over by it is not an option, so just turn it into a steppingstone. People depend on us; we know women are the heart of the household. Do it for your family no matter what comes at you.

I hope my story inspires you to become a *sur-thriver* and embark on your legacy. I never had the luxury of being able to quit. Too many people depend on me. I have surprised myself many times when crises happened in my life. I do not give any thought or any time to "What if I can't? What if I fail?" I only give my attention to "I have to try."

I always pray before I speak, "Give me the words to speak today that the people need to hear, even if it changes just one life." If I can do it, you can do it. Believe and take the first step. I look forward to hearing about your achievements. You can connect with me via social media, and maybe someday you too will be a Living Legend Honoree at a future Live Your Legacy Summit.

In Conclusion

"I cannot do everything, but still I can do something."
—Helen Keller

Do you feel inspired and energized by the stories in this book? I hope so, and I hope you start today to use these techniques outlined here to raise your power level and increase the joy and satisfaction in your life. Please join together with other women and men to change the world for the better. All the power in the world means nothing unless we use it to help others. I firmly believe the best focus for helping the world at this point in history is to lift up women and girls. As Rebecca Tinsley says:

"In modern war, women are deliberately targeted for systematic rape and abuse, because by destroying the will of women, you shatter their society. By the same measure, if you wish a community to recover and rebuild, you must empower the women and girls, because it is on their shoulders that responsibility rests."

So, take another woman's hand and take a stand for yourself, for your daughters, for a world that needs a woman's touch.

"One woman can change anything;
many women can change everything."
—Christine Karumba
Women for Women International's Country Director
for the Democratic Republic of Congo Chapter

About the Contributing Writers

More information and interviews with the contributors are at WomenConnect4Good.org.

Kristin Andress

If you rest on your laurels for long in life or business, Kristin Andress is bound to ask you, "How is that working for you?" She is on a perpetual quest to create the "What's Next?"

Kristin worked as Arthur Andersen's Director of Tax and Legal Performance and Learning, managing a multimillion-dollar budget, a global team of seventy-five people, and directed development and implementation of international programs for which she traveled extensively.

After a decade, she rejected the road warrior lifestyle, exited her successful career, took two years off to write books, and started Andress Strategy Consulting. She has worked with high-profile individuals and brands providing the strategy and vision necessary to launch new products, relaunch existing products, expand business portfolios, and position individuals as global experts. She believes everyone is accessible . . . if you have an offer, pure intention, and authenticity.

Kristin is a partner in RealizeX and VarsityQuad, companies offering developmental content to people who wish to engage in a more fulfilling life. She is also the president of Legacy Wisdom, an entity of the business, Legends & Legacy.

Her bestselling coauthored book, *Imagine Being in a Life You Love*, provides an invitation and rallying cry for people to design their lives by choice rather than leave it to chance. Kristin has been interviewed on national TV and radio and is a sought-after speaker for corporations globally.

Kristin earned a bachelor's degree in Public Communication/ Human Relations from Western Illinois University and a master's degree in Organizational Communications from the University of Missouri-Columbia. Kristin is dedicated to promoting animal rights and actively participates in several charities.

KristinAndress.com

ImagineBeing.com

Cheryl Benton

Cheryl Benton is founder and publisher of *The Three Tomatoes*, a free e-newsletter and lifestyle website for "women who aren't kids." The subscriber base numbers in the thousands. Topics in this insider's guide to living, playing, and having fun range from "the age thing," to travel, restaurants and bars, fashion, beauty, entertainment, giving back, and anything else that happens to be "coursing through our hormonally charged brains."

After a successful thirty year career in the New York City advertising agency business, Cheryl conceived the *Three Tomatoes* concept because "Living and working in New York City in the land of size zero twenty-somethings, I was truly starting to feel like an invisible woman," says Benton. "Since no one else was noticing us, it became apparent we were just going to have to take charge ourselves."

Cheryl also operates her own marketing consulting firm, 747 Marketing, which serves start-ups as well as *Fortune* 500 companies. Cheryl is a graduate of Adelphi University and a recipient of the "Distinguished Alumni Award." She is also a board member of the U.S. National Committee for UN Women, a United Nations NGO, and past president of the New York chapter, a board member of the New York Women's

Agenda (NYWA), and a board member of California Women's Conference. She was inducted into the Business Marketing Hall of Fame and is a frequent speaker on marketing to women and on women's global issues. A wife, mother, and grandmother, she resides in New York with her husband and two dogs.

747marketing.com
thethreetomatoes.com
twitter.com/The3tomatoes
facebook.com/thethreetomatoes

Claire Damken Brown, PhD

Dr. Claire Damken Brown, founder and president of Damken Brown and Associates, Inc., is a savvy speaker, industry consultant, and seminar leader specializing in diversity and equal employment opportunity strategies, gender communication, sexual harassment prevention, and cultural competency. Dr. Brown has twenty-five years of experience in *Fortune* 500 companies, featuring sixteen years at AT&T, and then Lucent Technologies directing diversity-related organizations, investigating discrimination cases globally, and training professionals. Her doctorate degree focused on male/female workplace communication.

She enjoys consulting nationally with corporations, agencies, and communities to build inclusive leadership skills and harassment-free work environments. As an adjunct professor at Metropolitan State College, she engages students in hot topics when teaching the Management Department's Workforce Diversity and Human Resource Management courses. Claire volunteers as the Diversity Director for the Colorado Society for Human Resource Management (SHRM) state council. She is the coauthor of three books: *Conflict and Diversity*, Hampton Press,

1997; *Code Switching: How to Talk So Men Will Listen*, Alpha Books/Penguin, 2009; and, *The Gender Communication Handbook: Conquering Conversational Collisions Between Men and Women*, Pfeiffer/Wiley, 2012.

DamkenBrown.com

Courtesy of Matt Spencer Photography

M. Bridget Cook-Burch

M. Bridget Cook-Burch is the *New York Times* and *Wall Street Journal* bestselling author best known for riveting tales of transformation. Her gift is her courage to bring light into the darkest places of humanity, and illuminating paths that awaken readers to their own magnificent journey. Her powerful work has been showcased on *Oprah*, CNN, *Good Morning America*, and in *People*, among others. Coauthor of bestselling *Shattered Silence, the Untold Story of a Serial Killer's Daughter* with Melissa G. Moore, and *Skinhead Confessions: From Hate to Hope* with former neo-Nazi TJ Leyden, Bridget's stories continue to rock readers around the world. Bridget's 2013 book, *The Witness Wore Red*, tells the astonishing life story of a woman who escaped from Warren Jeffs and the insidious organized crime ring of the FLDS church; and who has become a powerful advocate for the dignity of victims of human trafficking worldwide.

In writing, as in life, Bridget loves to refute stereotypes. After operating two transportation companies, she is now writing, speaking, and training full-time as CEO of Inspired Legacy, LLC. Bridget enjoys her four amazing children and more pets than her beloved husband can handle. An internationally sought-after speaker and activist, Bridget wows audiences on the subjects of radical transformation, conscious business, and how to leave the footprints of an inspired legacy.

BridgetInspires.com

facebook.com/pages/M-Bridget-Cook-Author-Speaker/256304737732646

twitter.com/inspiritwriter

Courtesy of Joe Orecchio

Vivian Diller, PhD

Vivian Diller, PhD, is a clinical psychologist in private practice in New York. Before receiving her doctorate, Vivian danced professionally with the Cincinnati Ballet company and was a Wilhelmina model. She received her PhD from Albert Einstein College of Medicine, interned at St. Luke's-Roosevelt Hospital and completed Postdoctoral Training in Psychoanalysis at NYU. For over twenty years, Vivian has researched the psychology of aging in contemporary culture, with a specific interest in women's self-image as they age. Her book, written with Michele Willens, *Face It: What Women Really Feel As Their Looks Change*, is now in paperback and translated around the world. Vivian has a column online at *Huffington Post* and *Psychology Today* and serves as a regular media expert about lifestyle issues on TV, radio, and the Internet. She consults for health and beauty companies, including Estée Lauder, P&G, Unilever, and Kimberly-Clark. Vivian is married to John Jacobs, MD, with whom she shares four children and two grandchildren.

VivianDiller.com
FaceItTheBook.com

Courtesy of *maryannerussell.com*

Gloria Feldt

Gloria Feldt is the cofounder and president of Take the Lead, an initiative to prepare, develop, inspire, and propel women to take their fair and equal share of leadership positions across all sectors by 2025. Take the Lead provides training, mentoring, role model programs, and thought leadership to companies, women's groups, and individuals.

The bestselling author of *No Excuses: Nine Ways Women Can Change How We Think about Power*, and three other books, she began her journey as a teen mom and high school dropout from rural Texas, then used her experience to become president and CEO of the world's largest reproductive health and advocacy organization, Planned Parenthood Federation of America. Her passion is to remove the last remaining obstacle to leadership parity: women's learned resistance to embracing their own power. This resistance is why women are stuck at 18 percent of top leadership positions and why the loss of high-performing female employees keeps organizations from optimal success. Chosen by *Vanity Fair* as one of America's top 200 women leaders, legends, and trailblazers, *Glamour* Woman of the Year, and one of Women's eNews 21 Leaders for the 21st Century,

Gloria teaches "Women, Power, and Leadership" at Arizona State University and inspires both men and women with her keynotes and Power Tool workshops. On her website she writes a popular blog, *Heartfeldt*. She has appeared on most national network and cable shows and as a commentator has been published in major media including the *New York Times*, the *Daily Beast*, *Salon*, *ForbesWoman*, and *Huffington Post*, and says she hangs out on social media far too much.

GloriaFeldt.com
twitter.com/GloriaFeldt
facebook.com/GloriaFeldt
linkedin.com/in/GloriaFeldt

Lois P. Frankel, PhD

Dr. Lois Frankel, president of Corporate Coaching International, a Pasadena, California, consulting firm, literally wrote the book on coaching people to succeed in businesses large and small around the globe. Her books, *Nice Girls Don't Get the Corner Office*, *Nice Girls Don't Get Rich*, and *Nice Girls Just Don't Get It* (coauthored with Carol Frohlinger), are international bestsellers translated into over twenty-five languages worldwide. *See Jane Lead* is a must-read for women who want to step confidently and courageously into the leadership zone. *Nice Girls Still Don't Get the Corner Office*, an updated tenth anniversary edition, was released in early 2014.

Sought after as a public speaker for her witty, warm, and practical presentations, Lois is among the top names of international speakers. She has appeared on the *Today Show*, *Larry King Live*, and *Fox News*, and has been featured in numerous newspapers and magazines. *Drop Dead Diva* creator, Josh Berman, has optioned the rights to all three Nice Girls' books for a comedy series.

Her clients number in the hundreds, and the list reads like a *Who's Who* of major multinational corporations. Lois founded two nonprofit organizations, MOSTE: Motivating Our Students Through Experience and Bloom Again Foundation. Her many honors include the Maybelline Women Who Empower Through Education award, the Los Angeles County Commission for Women's Woman of the Year award, a Presidential Medal from SUNY Oswego, and in addition to her earned doctorate from the University of Southern California, a Doctorate of Humane Letters from Phillips Graduate Institute.

drloisfrankel.com

Courtesy of Colleen Noonan

Joanna L. Krotz

A widely published journalist and entrepreneur, Joanna L. Krotz is the founder of The Woman's Playbook, a multimedia platform to encourage and support women's entrepreneurship that includes a web radio show, upcoming book, workshops, speaking, and content partnerships: Because being equal doesn't mean being the same.

Joanna is expert at mapping women's changing terrain on Wall Street and Main Street. At *Money* magazine, she pioneered groundbreaking coverage that tracked and celebrated women's growing financial muscle as consumers and investors. As an editor and columnist for print and digital small business media, including MSN, Joanna helped to increase the flow of capital and credibility for women-owned companies. She has interviewed and advised hundreds of women practitioners, coaches, and CEOs across the country about woman-charged issues, including finances, work-life balance, technology, growth strategies, and purpose marketing. At *Town&Country* magazine, Joanna again broke new ground by documenting women's characteristic choices about wealth, legacies, and charitable giving. She has been commissioned by clients as diverse as Microsoft, the

University of Indiana, and the U.S. State Department to examine small business, philanthropy, and leadership through a gender lens.

Joanna is editorial director of Muse2Muse Productions, a New York boutique content provider and author of *The Guide to Intelligent Giving: Make a Difference in the World and in Your Own Life*; *Making Philanthropy Count: How Women Are Changing the World*; and coauthor of *The Microsoft Small Business Kit*, a 500-page guide to entrepreneurship.

Joanna Krotz's work on behalf of women, entrepreneurship, and giving are helping to remake society's image and expectations of women and wealth.

The Woman's Playbook: *womansplaybook.com*

The Woman's Playbook podcasts on iTunes

muse2muse.com

joannakrotz.com

twitter.com/JoannaLKrotz

Google+/Joanna L. Krotz The Woman's Playbook

facebook.com/womansplaybook

linkedin.com/Joanna L Krotz

Courtesy of Anne Rich Photography

Aurea McGarry

Aurea McGarry is the Emmy Winning TV Show Host-Creator-Executive Producer of the *Live Your Legacy* TV series seen on PBS and Ion Television. She is also the founder and host of Live Your Legacy Summit, a national event series, a radio show host, speaker, author, bestselling coauthor, professional emcee, Mrs. U.S. Beauty of Georgia 2003, and cancer and domestic violence sur-thriver!

At the peak of a successful twenty-year sales career, Aurea was diagnosed with non-Hodgkin lymphoma on her birthday in 1999. After surgery and life-threatening chemotherapy, the surgeon told her she would never be able to speak above a faint whisper because they had to remove a major nerve to her vocal cord. The surgeon also removed half of her left lung, part of her right lung, the lining around her heart, her thymus gland and disconnected half of her diaphragm.

Cancer-free since 2000, Aurea wrote a book telling of that struggle and others in her life, called, *I Won't Survive . . . I'll Thrive*! As a six-time TV award winner, she has been a featured guest on over two-dozen TV news shows nationwide, *The 700 Club* worldwide TV broadcast, and over 200 radio shows worldwide. She travels the country speaking her message of faith, hope, laughter, and success to inspire others to overcome any obstacle in order to live their legacy now.

liveyourlegacysummit.com
liveyourlegacysummit@gmail.com
twitter.com/AureaMcGarry
facebook.com/aurea.mcgarry

Lisa Mininni

Lisa Mininni is the bestselling author of *Me, Myself, and Why? The Secrets to Navigating Change*, the president of Excellerate Associates, and the show host of Blog Talk Radio's *Navigating Change*. She released numerous eBooks, including *Get More Clients Now! 3 Steps to More Clients, More Money, and a Business You Love* available at *ExcellerateAssociates.com*. Lisa is a prominent business change and systems expert.

Known in over eleven countries, Lisa's expertise is sought out and featured on radio shows across the globe. Her articles on hardwiring and lead generation have been published on notable and respected sites, such as *Huffington Post*, *CareerBuilder*, and *RainToday*, and have achieved the Reader's Choice Award.

She is a Master Certified Business Coach (MCBC) through B/Coach Systems, Inc. and earned her Master of Business Administration through Central Michigan University.

As a strategist, she uses her strong twenty-year background in the world of organizational development as well as systems and quality improvement to show entrepreneurs and organizations how to systematize and monetize their mission and their message.

Lisa believes "when you work in alignment with who you are, it's not work." There is a flow to every business—when you discover your flow, you're energized and you attract opportunities from expected and unexpected sources . . . effortlessly.

Having systems in place simply makes it easy to bring in a consistent supply of prequalified prospects and turn them into clients up to 98 percent of the time.

linkedin.com/lisamininni
facebook.com/excellerateassociates
twitter.com/lisamininni

Courtesy of Dan Emrie

Nancy D. O'Reilly, PsyD

As a clinical psychologist, and founder of WomenSpeak.com, Nancy D. O'Reilly, PsyD, devotes her energies to helping women claim their power. Her lively, humorous, and engaging presentations educate and inspire audiences on the subjects of empowerment, succeeding in a multigenerational workplace, resiliency, mental toughness, mentoring, and connecting for good.

Dr. Nancy has a unique combination of life and growth experiences. She authored the self-help book *Timeless Women Speak: Feeling Youthful at Any Age*, based on her research with more than 1,200 women. Her publishing and radio careers, community activism, longstanding philanthropy, many honors and awards, and her outreach as a public speaker have given her a unique perspective on what women can accomplish in the world today.

Dr. Nancy consistently seeks out smart amazing women who nurture power and growth in themselves and others. In all her work she emphasizes the importance of owning one's power and using it to help others. She holds up a vision of how women are shaping the world into a better place. As a Nationally Certified

Crisis Team Leader, she served in New York City after 9/11, in Louisiana after Hurricane Katrina, and in Joplin after the devastating tornado. She has spent years helping people reclaim their power after weather disasters, fire, divorce, health crises, and job loss.

Nancy is also the founder of the 501(c)3 Women Connect4Good Foundation, which seeks to educate women to participate in social-profit activities and improve their careers, finances, health, and relationships. She received a Missourian Award in 2010; has chaired a United Way Women's Initiative; and participated in the 2011 United Nations Commission on the Status of Women. She serves on many boards, including the Missouri State Committee of Psychologists Board of Directors.

drnancy@womenspeak.com
twitter.com/drnancyoreilly
facebook.com/WomenSpk
womenconnect4good.org

Shirley Osborne

Shirley Osborne is the CEO of Posh Affairs, Inc. Shirley's work leads her into the lives of girls and women in many parts of the world, in the quest to realize her personal and professional vision: "Every girl succeeds. Everybody wins."

Shirley holds a master's degree in Business Administration from Simmons College, Boston, and has contributed her skills and passion in partnership with organizations on behalf of women and children. She has reported on the United Nations General Assembly Special Sessions for Women, been a listener with World Pulse, and facilitated online discussions for UNIFEM (now, UN Women) and MTV. Shirley is a facilitator with the World Academy for the Future of Women and an organizer with the International Women's Day global planning organizations.

Her articles have been published in *Caribbean Life*, the *Jamaica Gleaner* and the *Montserrat Reporter* among others, and she is the author of *Tolerance Is No Virtue: Ignorance, Appreciation and the Human Story* and, most recently, *Your Soul Is Gold: Mine It.*

In her other moments, Shirley is an avid sailor, hiker, and traveler who dances often, loves cricket, big cities, and being chef to close friends. She lives for family get-togethers on Montserrat, her Caribbean island home, enjoys the deserts of Arizona, and is committed to protecting the oceans of the world.

fasolanews.com
femininealchemy.com
twitter.com/falchemist
twitter.com/fasola5
facebook.com/FA-SO-La

Courtesy of Helene Glassman

Lois Phillips, PhD

Lois Phillips, PhD, is a speaker, educator, college administrator, consultant, trainer, and coach. She has received numerous honors and awards for her work as a community and professional leader, based in her belief that communication is an essential skill for personal and organizational success. Speakers become leaders when they can inspire change in others through effective public speaking, personal presence, being an example of trustworthiness, and demonstrating competence and EQ (Emotional Intelligence or Quotient).

Lois works with diverse women and men, helping them brave the risks of speaking up. She trains them in relating their message to an audience using techniques including the use of PowerPoint technology, demonstrating passion for an issue, personality traits such as trustworthiness and wit, as well as the use of appropriate storytelling narratives and self-disclosure.

In 2006, Lois published *Women Seen and Heard: Lessons Learned from Successful Speakers* with coauthor, Dr. Anita Perez Ferguson. Since then, she has facilitated Communication and Strategic Planning Skills workshops, coached "C" level executives and political advocates, and spoken about the importance of public speaking skills to Mid-Career Women at the JFK School, Babson College MBA Alumni, and Professional Women's Association at the University of California Santa Barbara.

Lois was the founding director and CEO of Antioch University Santa Barbara where she was also a faculty member for eleven years. During that time, she completed her doctoral studies at the University of California. A community leader, she was a founding member and president of many community boards and committees and a frequent media commentator on women's issues.

loisphillips.com
facebook.com/lois.phillips
twitter.com/loisphillips

Courtesy of Annie Holt

Birute Regine, EdD

Birute Regine, EdD, is an executive and life coach, group facilitator, consultant, public speaker, and founder of Iron Butterfly Power Circles. She coauthored the critically acclaimed book, renamed in paperback as, *Weaving Complexity and Business: Engaging the Soul at Work.* Her latest book, *Iron Butterflies: Women Transforming Themselves and the World,* won the Nautilus Book Awards silver medal in 2011 in both social change and women's interest categories. Over a period of several years, Birute interviewed sixty women from all walks of life from eight countries. She coined the phrase "Iron Butterflies" for these dynamic role models to describe how they meld a will of iron with the gentle, nurturing touch of a butterfly. She has since developed Iron Butterfly Circles in which women support other women through relationships that nurture and develop their inherent strengths. She blogs for *Huffington Post* and *Forbes* and dedicates herself to enhancing feminine power at work and in the world.

A Harvard-educated developmental psychologist, Birute was a project manager at the Harvard Project of the Psychology of Women and Development of Girls headed by the psychologist

Carol Gilligan. She was also a visiting scholar at the Research Center of Women at Wellesley College; an affiliate of the Stone Center founded by Jean Baker Miller; and a member of the complexity research group at the London School of Economics.

ironbutterflies.com
facebook/ironbutterflies
twitter.com/ironbutterflies

Courtesy of Angela Tellman

Linda Rendleman

Linda Rendleman, MS, is cofounder of the Women Like Us Foundation, a not-for-profit worldwide organization that supports women-led causes that are changing the world and engages women and girls to make a difference globally and locally. She is also the creator of the Women Like Us book series.

Her book *Women Like Us: Real Stories and Strategies for Living Your Best Life*, 2008, is the namesake for the foundation. Linda's most recent book, *Women Like Us Illuminating the World: Real Stories, Real Strategies*, focuses on the work of women creating change and coaches the reader to find her own path for giving back.

Linda is an award-winning speaker and an author who focuses on sharing motivating and uplifting strategies to support women to be the best that they can be. She is also the founder of Business Women Connect, an award-winning networking company for women, and has hosted her own television and radio shows.

With a degree in public speaking from Indiana University and a degree in counseling from Butler University, she has devoted her life's work to giving back to others and sharing her own personal story of empowerment. Through her foundation women can invest in other women through cultural immersion, teen mentoring programs, and support of women-led causes.

lindarendleman.com
facebook.com/linda.rendleman.5
twitter.com/lindarendleman
womenlikeusfoundation.org

Courtesy of Tina Celle

Marcia Reynolds, PsyD

Dr. Marcia Reynolds, president of Covisioning LLC, is considered an expert on how the brain works. In addition to coaching leaders and top talent in multinational companies, she travels the world speaking at conferences and teaching classes in leadership, coaching, and emotional intelligence

Prior to starting her own business, Marcia's greatest success came when she helped to transform a semiconductor manufacturer from near-bankruptcy to the #1 stock-market success when it went public in 1993. Marcia's employee development program focused on inspiring a positive mindset and empowering cross-functional teams to become the heart of the organization.

Excerpts from her books, *Outsmart Your Brain* and *Wander Woman: How High-Achieving Women Find Contentment and Direction*, have appeared in many places including *Harvard Management Review*, Forbes.com, CNN.com, *Psychology Today*, and the *New York Times*; and she has appeared on *ABC World News*.

Marcia's doctoral degree is in organizational psychology with a research emphasis on high-achieving women in today's corporations. As a founding member of the International Coach

Federation and one of the first twenty-five people in the world to become a Master Certified Coach, she is a true pioneer in the coaching profession. She is also the training director for the Healthcare Coaching Institute.

This article is excerpted with permission from *Wander Woman: How High-Achieving Women Find Contentment and Direction*, by Marcia Reynolds, Berrett-Koehler, June 2010. There are exercises and strategies outlined in the book to help women navigate the journey from stress to significance.

psychologytoday.com/blog/wander-woman
outsmartyourbrain.com/

Courtesy of Kate Szamari

Marci Shimoff

Marci Shimoff is a #1 *New York Times* bestselling author, a celebrated transformational leader, and one of the nation's leading experts on happiness, success, and unconditional love. She is the author of *Love for No Reason* and *Happy for No Reason*, which offer revolutionary approaches to experiencing deep and lasting love and happiness.

Marci is also the woman's face of the biggest self-help book phenomenon in history, with six bestselling titles in the series, including *Chicken Soup for the Woman's Soul* and *Chicken Soup for the Mother's Soul*. In total, her books have sold more than 15 million copies worldwide, have been on the *New York Times* bestseller list for 118 weeks, and translated into thirty-three languages. She hosts the national PBS television show *Happy for No Reason* and is a featured teacher in the international film and book phenomenon *The Secret*.

President and cofounder of the Esteem Group, Marci is a frequent keynote speaker, a top-rated trainer for *Fortune* 500 companies, and a sought-after media interview. She earned her MBA from UCLA and an advanced certificate in stress management consulting. She is a founding member and board member of the Transformational Leadership Council, which serves over 20 million people. She considers her life's purpose to be helping people live more empowered and joy-filled lives.

This piece is adapted with permission from *Love for No Reason: 7 Steps to Creating a Life of Unconditional Love*, Free Press, 2010. *Love for No Reason* offers a breakthrough approach to experiencing a lasting state of unconditional love—the kind of love that doesn't depend on another person, situation, or romantic partner, and that you can access at any time and in any circumstance. This is the key to lasting joy and fulfillment in life.

TheLoveBook.com

twitter.com/Marci_Shimoff

Courtesy of Margaret McQusiton

Rebecca Tinsley

Rebecca Tinsley founded the human rights group Waging Peace following a visit to the refugee camps in Darfur, Sudan. She also founded Network for Africa to help survivors of genocide rebuild their lives. Network for Africa has schools and clinics in Rwanda and Uganda.

Rebecca is a former BBC reporter and writes about Africa, women, genocide, and human rights. Her book, *When the Stars Fall to Earth: A Novel of Africa*, is available on Amazon.

Together with her husband, Henry, she was asked by President and Mrs. Carter to start the Carter Center in Europe. She is on the advisory councils of Bennington College, Vermont, and Antioch University in Santa Barbara, California. Rebecca splits her time between California, London, and Africa.

RebeccaTinsley.com
Network4Africa.org
facebook/beckytinsley
twitter/beckytinsley

Courtesy of Linda Wilson

Sandra Ford Walston

Sandra Ford Walston, The Courage Expert, is the principal of a twenty-year-old leadership-consulting firm based in Denver, Colorado. She is a trailblazer in the field of the feminine behaviors of courage and nongender courageous leadership. Featured as a witty, provocative, concrete, and insightful speaker, she has sparked positive changes in the lives of thousands of leaders each year. Sandra also provides skills-based training programs for some of the most respected public and private blue-chip businesses and organizations in the world.

With over twenty years of experience with finance professionals, she instructs for the University of Denver and formerly taught for the Colorado Society of CPAs. She is certified in both the Myers-Briggs Type Indicator and the Enneagram, a powerful tool for understanding the personality patterns that affect our lives.

Sandra has been published in several magazines and has written three books. Internationally published *COURAGE: The Heart and Spirit of Every Woman/Reclaiming the Forgotten Virtue* and *The COURAGE Difference at Work: A Unique Success Guide for Women* (formerly *STUCK*) merge more than twenty years of courage research to reveal how workplace obstacles keep women at all levels stuck and how specific courage actions can be applied to step up the leadership ladder. Her third, nongender book, *FACE IT! 12 Actions That Bring Success at Work and Beyond* confirms that what holds you back on the job is the same as what hinders achievement—the reluctance to face and live a courageous life.

sandrawalston.com

twitter.com/CourageExpert

facebook.com/courageexpert

linkedin.com/in/sandrafordwalston

facebook.com/sandra.ford.walston

youtube.com/user/Courageexpert/

Courtesy of Wendy Kout

Michele Willens

Michele Willens is a journalist, author, and playwright who coined the term "tweens" for the *New York Times*. She is a regular contributor to the *Huffington Post*, the *Atlantic*, and the *Daily Beast*; and edited *FACE IT: What Women Really Feel As Their Looks Change*. Her most recent theatrical piece was *Waiting for Dr. Hoffman*, a one-act play about four women who meet in the waiting room of a cosmetic surgeon's office. She is married, has two children, and lives in New York City.

FaceItTheBook.com

Courtesy of Niki May Day Photography

Janet Rose Wojtalik, EdD

Dr. Janet Rose Wojtalik attributes her adult professional pursuits to the career-option limitations placed on her, and all girls, when she was a child. As a child her career path was based on the typical expectation for girls: she was expected to become a teacher. Besides teaching school, Janet became an author, motivational speaker, and school administrator. Her eBook, *The Seven Secrets of Parenting Girls*, is available online and serves as a valuable parent resource for nurturing female leadership. She has also authored the Strong Girls series, a collection of children's books with messages of independence, hardiness, and open career options for young girls. Her most recent work, *Raising Successful Women from Childhood to Womanhood*, provides a workbook for parents.

Janet earned her doctorate in educational leadership from Duquesne University. Her research about women and leadership won her a Clark Scholar designation in the 2006 David L. Clark National Graduate Research Seminar in San Francisco, California. Her research propelled her to become a resource as a parenting expert with a national speaking platform. She is the director of Student Support Services for the Fairview

School District in Pennsylvania and an adjunct professor at two Pennsylvania universities.

janet@drjanetrose.com
parentinggirls.com
blog.parentinggirls.com

Resources

Resources are grouped under the essay in which they are referenced.

"From Oppression to Leadership: Women Redefine Power," by Gloria Feldt

"The Equal Rights Amendment." U.S. History Pre-Columbian to the New Millenium.

www.businesswire.com/news/home/20120321005131/en/Women-Owned-BusinessesLeaders-Job-Creation-Revenue-Growth. March 21, 2012.

"By the numbers: Women's progress (or not) around the world." CNN.com.

Profile of Sheryl Sandberg. forbes.com/profile/sheryl-sandberg.

The Representation Project, formerly MisRepresentation .org.

Rosin, Hanna. *The End of Men: And the Rise of Women*. New York: The Penguin Group, 2012.

Sandberg, Sheryl. "Why We Have Too Few Women Leaders." TEDTalk Women, Dec. 2010.

Smith, Stacy L., PhD, and Marc Choueiti. "Gender Disparity on Screen and Behind the Camera in Family Films." Annenberg School for Communication & Journalism, University of Southern California.

"The Status of Women in U.S. Media 2013." Women's Media Center.

"The Power of the Podium: Challenges and Opportunities to Be Seen and Heard," by Lois Phillips, PhD

http://catalyst.org/knowledge/2013-catalyst-census-fortune-500.

Easterbrook, Gregg. *Sonic Boom: Globalization at Mach Speed.* New York: Random House, 2009.

Ehrenreich, Barbara. "Public Freaking." *Ms. Magazine.* September 1989, 40–41.

Grabe, Maria Elizabeth, and Lelia Samson. "Sexual Cues Emanating from the Anchorette Chair: Implications for Perceived Professionalism, Fitness for Beat, and Memory for News." Indiana University: *Sage Journals.*

www.hbr.org/2013/01/the-best-performing-ceos-in-the-world.

Lombrozo, Tania. "Speaking Out about Women and Power." *Cosmos & Culture,* February 4, 2013.

www.npr.org/blogs/ombudsman/2010/04/where_are_the_women.

www.nydailynews.com/entertainment/tv-moviesfox-anchor-suspended-calling-rachel-maddow-angry-young-man.

"Podiumitis (An Extremely Common Though Rarely Discussed Affliction)." *Santa Barbara News-Press.* August 29, 1999, J-1.

www.she-conomy.com/facts-on-women.

Tannen, Deborah, PhD. *You Just Don't Understand: Women and Men in Conversation.* New York: Harper Collins, 2007.

www.usatoday.com/story/news/world/2013/01/23clinton-congressional-hearing-testimony-libya/1859433/.

"Power Up! Three Ways to Build Credibility and Make Yourself Heard," by Claire Damken Brown, PhD

Brown, Claire Damken, and Audrey Nelson. *Code Switching: How to Talk So Men Will Listen.* New York: Alpha/Penguin, 2009, 38, 40, 74–77.

Gamble, Teri Kwai, and Michael Gamble. *The Gender Communication Connection.* Boston: Houghton Mifflin, 2003, 78–79.

Mindell, Phyllis. *A Woman's Guide to the Language of Success: Communicating with Confidence and Power.* Englewood Cliffs, NJ: Prentice Hall, 1995, 105.

Nelson, Audrey, and Claire Damken Brown. *The Gender Communication Handbook: Conquering Conversational Collisions Between Men and Women.* San Francisco: Pfeiffer/Wiley, 2012, 68–70.

Popken, Ben. "For Marissa Mayer, It's God, family and Yahoo." *www.today.com/parents.* Accessed 11-28-2012.

Tannen, Deborah. *Talking from 9 to 5: How Women's and Men's Conversational Styles Affect Who Gets Heard, Who Gets Credit, and What Gets Done at Work.* New York: William Morrow, 1994, 232–33.

"U.S. Women in Business." Catalyst Knowledge Center, 2012.

West, Candace. "When the Doctor Is a 'Lady': Power, Status and Gender in Physician-Patient Encounters." In J. Coates (Ed.), *Language and Gender: A Reader.* Malden, MA: Blackwell, 1998, 397.

Wood, Julia. "Mentoring to Support Women." *Gendered Lives: Communication, Gender and Culture.* 6th ed. Belmont, CA: Wadsworth, 2005, 122.

"Eight Key Ways Women Become Natural and Necessary Leaders," by Lois P. Frankel, PhD

Frankel, Lois P. *See Jane Lead: 99 Ways to Take Charge at Work*. New York: Grand Central Publishing, 2009.

"Soft Is the New Hard: The Hidden Power of Feminine Skills," by Birute Regine, EdD

Brittingham, Jean. "Women and Collective Intelligence Will Solve Our Planetary Crises." *Fast Company*. (Undated)

Doyle, Anne. "What Makes Teams Smarter?" Forbes.com. June 20, 2011.

Woolley, Anita W., Christopher F. Chabris, Alex Pentland, Nada Hashmi, and Thomas W. Malone. "Evidence for a Collective Intelligence Factor in the Performance of Human Groups." *Science Magazine*. October 29, 2010, Vol. 330 no. 6004: 686–88.

Woolley, Anita, and Thomas Malone. "Defend Your Research: What Makes a Team Smarter? More Women." *Harvard Business Review*. June, 2011.

"How Women Can Hit the Bull's-Eye with Courage (Every Time)," by Sandra Ford Walston

Da Costa, René. "Simple Courage." Management-Issues .com. October 13, 2005.

Tolle, Eckhart. *The Power of Now.* Novato, CA: New World Library, 1999, 35.

"The Burden of Greatness," by Marcia Reynolds, PsyD

Ruderman, Marian N., and Patricia J. Ohlott. *Standing at the Crossroads: Next Steps for High-Achieving Women.* San Francisco: Jossey-Bass, 2002. 120–21.

Wagner, Ina, and Ruth Wodak. (Examples of ways women are rewriting their definitions of success.) "Performing success: Identifying strategies of self-presentation in women's biographical narratives." *Discourse & Society.* 2006: 17(3). 406–07.

"The New Beauty Paradox," by Vivian Diller, PhD, with Michele Willens

Aharon, Itzhak, and Nancy Etcoff, et al. "Beautiful Faces Have Variable Reward Value." *Neuron* 32, no. 3 (November 8, 2001): 537–51.

Cowley, Geoffrey. "The Biology of Beauty." *Newsweek* 127 (1996): 60–67.

Etcoff, Nancy, et al. "The Real Truth about Beauty: A Global Report." Commissioned by Dove, a Unilever Beauty Brand. September 2004.

Fox, Kate. "Mirror, Mirror." A Summary of Research Findings on Body Image. *Social Issues Research Centre*, 1997.

Maestripieri, Dario. "Developmental and Evolutionary Aspects of Female Attraction to Babies." *American Psychological Association*, no. 1, January 2004.

Miller, Arthur G. "Role of Physical Attractiveness in Impression Formation." *Psychonomic Science* 19, no. 4 (1970): 241–43.

Nisbett, Richard E., and Timothy DeCamp Wilson. "The Halo Effect: Evidence for Unconscious Alteration of Judgments," *Journal of Personality and Social Psychology* 35, no. 4 (1977): 250–56.

Samuels, C.A., et al. "Facial Aesthetics: Babies Prefer Attractiveness to Symmetry." *Perception* 23, no. 7 (1994): 823–31.

Hoover, Gina, and Daniel Arkkelin. "Can't Buy Me Love: Effects of Masculinity, Femininity, Commitment, Attractiveness, and Income on Friendship, Dating, and Marriage Choices," Valparaiso University, Paper presented at the annual meeting of the Midwestern Psychological Association, Chicago (2002).

About Take the Lead

Founded by financial industry success story Amy Litzenberger and women's advocate and leadership expert Gloria Feldt, Take the Lead is a 501(c)3 tax-exempt nonprofit organization with a mission to prepare, develop, inspire, and propel women to take their fair and equal share of leadership positions across all sectors by 2025. It's today's women's movement—a unique catalyst for women to embrace power and reach leadership parity.

Five percent of all publisher's proceeds from this book will be donated to Take the Lead.

For more information, visit: *www.TaketheLeadWomen.com.*

Index